Healing Through Communication

To my son David,
and to the memory of my mother,
Claire Harcourt Leppanen

Healing Through Communication

THE PRACTICE OF CARING

Carol Leppanen Montgomery

SAGE PUBLICATIONS
International Educational and Professional Publisher
Newbury Park   London   New Delhi

For information address:

SAGE Publications, Inc.
2455 Teller Road
Newbury Park, California 91320

SAGE Publications Ltd.
6 Bonhill Street
London EC2A 4PU
United Kingdom

SAGE Publications India Pvt. Ltd.
M-32 Market
Greater Kailash I
New Delhi 110 048 India

Printed in the United States of America

Library of Congress Cataloging-in-Publication Data

Montgomery, Carol Leppanen.
   Healing through communication: the practice of caring / Carol Leppanen Montgomery.
    p.   cm.
   Includes bibliographical references and index.
   ISBN 0-8039-5120-5 (cl.).—ISBN 0-8039-5121-3 (pbk.)
   1. Caring. 2. Medical personnel and patient. 3. Patients—Psychology. 4. Caregivers—Psychology. I. Title.
   [DNLM: 1. Communication. 2. Professional-Patient Relations.
   3. Caregivers—psychology. W 62 M7867h 1993]
   R727.3.M65 1993
   601.69′6—dc20
                                             93-12056

94 95 96 10 9 8 7 6 5 4

Sage Production Editor: Tara S. Mead

Contents

Preface

$\mathcal{A}$t one time, medical advances and technology seemed to promise deliverance from the threat of our own vulnerability and mortality. As Daniel Callahan once noted, however, this promise has yet to be fulfilled. Mortality rates are still the same as they have always been—one per person.

So, while science and technology still struggle to buffer the onslaughts of illness, debilitation, and death, these threats continue to be a part of our human existence, and we are still faced with our own mortality. We have controlled such scourges as polio and the whooping cough, but new plagues, such as cancer and AIDS, continue to touch the lives of most individuals. Even those who practice every preventive control strategy are not invulnerable, and none of us is immune from the threat of loss of our loved ones.

All we have left when control strategies fail us, and breakdown occurs, are the compassion and caring that we extend to one another. Unfortunately, during our fascination with the promise of technology, we lost sight of the importance of this human element.

In our culture, caring is viewed as frivolous compared to the real work of curing. Our cultural heros are those who represent power—the power to save us from the invisible demons that seem to cause our suffering. Yet each day, a very different form of heroics is shown by those who stand by and care for those for whom technology has failed: the disabled, the chronically ill, and the dying.

Our society shuns these victims, for they represent our failures and loss of control. As these victims are shunned, the efforts to help them create a meaningful existence are also ignored and devalued.

In this book, I would like to shed light on this underacknowledged, but very important, part of health care and to recognize caring as being more than mere sentiment. I will at least begin to address the complexity and depth of insight that is required of those professionals brave enough to get involved beyond their professional persona, and who use their hearts as well as their science to heal. It is my hope that this text will inspire caregivers to give a voice to and advocate for what Jean Watson would call the private and invisible world of a patient. I also hope that both students and seasoned clinicians will be reinspired to find meaning and joy in their work, as I have been reinspired by my work on this project.

The use of the terms *client* and *patient* was considered in terms of their implications. It has been fashionable in some disciplines to substitute the word *client* for *patient* because of the paternalistic implications of the role of the *patient* in the health-care system. On the other hand, the term *client* might seem artificial in some settings, because it seems to deny the vulnerability and special status afforded to those who are truly helpless. Therefore, both of these terms are used throughout this text, to represent both connotations of the experience of being a recipient of health-care services.

Acknowledgments

I am extremely grateful to Trish Jones, my dissertation chair, for her belief that scholarship should make a difference in the world. Her courage in taking risks and her unrelenting, but supportive rigor have been a great example. I also wish to thank the rest of my committee: Al Goldberg, Carl Larson, Karol Merten, and Janet Quinn. A postbaccalaureate training grant from the Division of Health and Human Services funded the dissertation research, and the research committee, through the Center for Nursing Research at the University of Colorado, funded the continuation. Joanie Rogers Jackson, Debby Sandella, Pauli Sarasoli, Kay Vaughn, and Denny Webster all provided helpful feedback about the manuscript and the developing theory.

The Center for Human Caring at the University of Colorado School of Nursing has provided intellectual stimulation, especially with the ideas of Peggy Chinn, Sally Gadow, Janet Quinn, and the founder, Jean Watson. Similarly, I wish I could acknowledge those countless students, workshop participants, and colleagues who stimulated my thinking and provided me with new ideas about caring.

Many nurses with whom I have worked in the past have taught me so much and made me proud to be a nurse. The two that stand out in my mind are Charlene Miller and Kay Davis. Recently, I had the good fortune to discover the work of Rachel Corday, an artist whose vision has helped me to appreciate caring and spirituality in a whole new way.

Finally, my most important debt of gratitude goes to the participants in this research. Their stories, their insights, and the sheer depth of their practice went far beyond what I had expected to find when I started this project. These individual caregivers are the heart and soul of this book.

Introduction

The Investigation of Caring

$\mathcal{T}$he purpose of this book is to offer a theory of caring that is grounded in clinical practice and is appropriate as a framework for communication in health care.

Because caring is not well represented in the theoretical literature, the logical approach to understanding this type of communication seemed to be to look within the realm of practice. My own interest in pursuing this research was motivated by my professional evolution during my 22 years of practice as a psychiatric nurse. While I was initially guided by the paradigms of psychology and medicine, I found that my practice eventually evolved to the point that it no longer fit within these frameworks. The emphasis on science and objectivity limited my capacities to be with clients in a way that I felt to be significant. Yet there was no dialogue or established theory with which to understand this more involved level of practice. Therefore, I often suppressed my instincts and my compassion in order to keep my practice within conventional boundaries. I was also struck by the fact that I was being affected by some of my clients in deeply

AUTHOR'S NOTE: Portions of this book have appeared previously in: *Common Boundary* (vol. 9:6) 1991; The *Journal of Transpersonal Psychology* (23:2) 1991; Gaut, D. (Ed.), *The Presence of Caring in Nursing*, New York: National League for Nursing Press.

significant ways, but I minimized these experiences because they fell outside of my realm of understanding.

In spite of these limitations, most of us who have worked with patients seem to know on some level that the only time we have really made a difference was when we were willing to get involved in a way that mattered to us as well as to our patients—a way that went beyond the boundaries of theories, science, or the treatment plan. We rarely talked about these experiences, however. When we spoke at a professional level in the psychiatric setting we were more objective. We related to patients and discussed treatment at the abstract level of theory and used the language that seemed to carry the most established power. Usually that was the language of medicine or of psychology.

In fact, compassion seemed to be viewed with suspicion in psychiatric settings and was interpreted as countertransference or as being manipulated by a patient. In medical settings, compassion seemed to be associated with emotionality and loss of objectivity and control.

Recently, however, theories have begun to emerge that give a language to a more subjective and intuitive level of understanding and healing. Feminist theorists (Belenky, Clinchy, Goldberger, & Tarule, 1986; Chodorow, 1978; Gilligan, 1982; Jordan, 1989; Miller, 1976; Noddings, 1984; and others) validate a way of understanding and of helping that emphasizes the importance of relationships, connections, feelings, and compassion. In addition, nursing theorists such as Watson (1985, 1988a, 1988b), Gadow (1985, 1988), Benner and Wrubel (1989), and Leininger (1981, 1984) validate caring as a central concept in nursing, and they have developed this concept at a theoretical level.

These authors reinforced and helped me understand what I had been aware of at an intuitive level, and they inspired me to want to study the communication of caring. I wanted to better understand the caring I had witnessed and been part of, and to make explicit this communication that seemed to be quietly going on in the background of clinical settings. In order to make this phenomenon explicit, I was determined to initiate the dialogue that was not being spoken in health-care settings. Therefore, I went to the exemplar caregivers and asked them to tell me about their experiences with caring.

I wanted to understand their responses to two questions: First, what is the nature of caring communication from the perspective of caregivers, and second, what is this experience like for each of them? Is caring associated with burnout, as some authors have claimed (Maslach, 1983), or is it associated with the professional rewards, as Benner (1984) has observed in relation to nursing. Because there was no widely used theory or specific language even to talk about caring at a conceptual level, I asked my informants to talk about caring in regard to examples or stories. I have found that anyone who has worked in health care has at least one story to tell, an experience with a patient that will always be with them. Therefore, I asked each of my informants to talk about an experience with caring that stood out for them.

The method that I used is *grounded theory* (Glaser & Strauss, 1967), a way to generate theory inductively from social data. This method was carried out within the assumptions of a qualitative naturalistic paradigm of inquiry, as described by Lincoln and Guba (1985). In keeping with the naturalistic view, my informants were assumed to be experts with regard to the questions I was asking.

A pilot study included my own involvement as a participant observer during an experience as a psychiatric consultation-liaison nurse in a general hospital. Within this role, I counseled patients experiencing behavioral or emotional distress while in the hospital, and I consulted with hospital staff to support them and to enhance their skills in working with these patients. Working in this role as researcher as well as clinician gave me the opportunity to witness caring as it unfolded in the distinctive context of the hospital environment, and to critique my own experiences as a direct caregiver.

A total of 45 health professionals participated in semistructured interviews in which they were asked to talk about experiences that stood out for them in terms of caring. Because of the elusiveness and complexity of the concept of caring, I began by focusing on just one group of health-care providers so that I could establish the essential qualities, or core categories of caring (Montgomery, 1990).

Nurses were selected as the initial sampling group because the nursing profession identifies care as the essence of the profession (Leininger, 1984; Watson, 1985), and an earlier pilot study revealed that nurses seemed to share a language and common understandings about caring that were helpful in the initial stage of the research. Once the core categories and the tentative theory were

established, sampling decisions were directed toward representing diverse groups of caregivers, such as occupational therapists,
physical therapists, speech pathologists, psychologists, social workers, counselors, and physicians, to determine whether the developing theory held up with these groups as well. The core elements
of caring seemed remarkably consistent, as represented by exemplars of caring across all of these disciplines.

The initial sampling plan included nurses who were nominated
by others as representing exemplars of caring, those who were
perceived as experts by their peers, according to Benner's (1984)
framework. In order to avoid developing a one-dimensional view
of caring, I wanted to compare and contrast those exemplar cases
with cases representing contrasting dimensions of caring, such as
those who (a) were not successful with caring, (b) had negative
satisfaction with caring, (c) had relatively less professional experience, and (d) had fewer opportunities for relational involvement
with patients.

The dimension of *nonsuccess with caring* was represented by
several nurses who worked in an intensive care unit (ICU) of a
publicly funded hospital that was described as being like a "war
zone." These nurses were referred by their manager as very caring
people; however, they often did not act that way in that setting.
These nurses seemed to have a love/hate relationship with their
work, and they expressed their frustration and anger caused by
the stress of the environment with inappropriate communication
behaviors. For example, some of them were very rigid with families about visiting hours, some had bizarre and sarcastic senses of
humor, and some got into trouble because of conflicts with the
resident physicians. This manager explained that all of these nurses
were quite caring and passionate about their work, but that the
setting was so chaotic and highly intense that they had to be tough
in order to survive. The interview confirmed that they did indeed
feel deep passion about their work, and all of them related incidents in which they had become deeply involved with a patient.
These nurses could clearly articulate why they had chosen to
distance themselves from such relationships, and they provided a
great deal of insight about why some caregivers emotionally disengage from their work.

Negative satisfaction with caring was represented by the aforementioned ICU nurses, but it was also a theme interwoven through

many of the sampling groups. Several caregivers from a variety of disciplines talked about different periods in their career when they had felt disillusioned with caring. One nurse who suffered posttraumatic stress syndrome following the death of a patient represented this dimension most vividly.

Relatively less professional experience was represented by four caregivers who had less than 5 years of experience in their field. In addition, many of the other experienced informants described situations that had occurred early in their careers.

The dimension of *fewer opportunities for relational involvement* was represented by professionals working with clients who were unable to participate fully in a relationship with a caregiver. For example, caregivers worked in settings with adults who were severely mentally retarded, suffering from dementia, or literally unconscious, such as during and after surgery, or even comatose.

The analysis of the data, by constant comparative analysis (Glaser & Strauss, 1967), produced a category system that describes the form of caring communication in a way that I hope will be helpful to guide beginning practitioners and will also serve as a source of refinement and inspiration for experts.

Part I of this text introduces the reader to the concept of caring. Chapter 1 explains the importance of caring in heath care. Chapter 2 grounds the concept of caring in existing theory in the fields of communication, nursing, philosophy, and feminist psychology.

Parts II and III are based on the findings of the research described in this introduction. Part II provides a descriptive theory of caring, each chapter representing a different dimension. Chapter 3 describes the predispositional qualities of the caregiver that are necessary for caring. Chapter 4 describes the behavioral manifestations of caring, and Chapter 5 looks at those elements of caring that are relational in nature. As this text shows, caring cannot be separated from its context; therefore, Chapter 6 describes unique qualities of the health-care environment that shape the communication of caring. This section concludes with Chapter 7, which distinguishes the deep involvement of caring from destructive forms of overinvolvement.

Part III looks at the effects of caring. Chapter 8 describes the transformative effects of caring on both the client and the caregiver, and Chapter 9 looks at the emotional risks of caring for the caregiver. Chapter 10 presents a model that describes the support necessary to sustain this level of communication and to help caregivers cope with the emotional demands of caring. Finally, Chapter 11 considers some final thoughts about caring and how to promote this type of communication in practice and educational settings.

Part I

The Concept of Caring

One

Putting the Caring
Back Into Health Care

$\mathcal{A}$ mother whose daughter was killed as a result of an automobile accident wrote an open letter to health professionals, which was published in the *Washington Post* (cited in Reilly, 1978):

> Please search yourselves for resources to deal helpfully with others like us. Seek ways to make the few moments available for deeply troubled persons times of healing rather than destruction. Plan ways of staffing your facilities with people who are full of heart and wise in the administration of compassion. We need caring so desperately. (p. v)

The word *caring* has been trivialized and even used as an advertising slogan for everything from doctors to laundry detergent; however, in health care, as the preceding testimony illustrates, caring cannot be trivialized. The purpose of this book is to offer a theory of caring that is grounded in clinical practice and is appropriate as a framework for communication in health care.

The Significance of Caring in Health Care

Caring is more important in health care now than it has ever been. Jean Watson (1988b) believes that we are moving "out of an

9

era in which *curing* is dominant into an era in which *caring* must take precedence" (p. 175). There are several reasons for this. First, the aging of the population and the decreased mortality rate from what were previously life-threatening illnesses have resulted in a prevalence of chronic conditions that cannot be cured. In fact, cure only occurs in about 10% of patients seen by physicians (Fuchs, 1975). The other 90% require supportive, caring interventions to facilitate their own coping and healing resources.

Another reason why caring is so important right now has to do with disillusionment with the modern health-care system and the limitations of the medical model. The medical model, which is the foundation of our current health-care system, is based on a mechanical view of the universe and the separation of mind from body, ideas that emerged from the scientific revolution of the past three centuries. Disease is seen as separate from the person and as a self-contained event, independent of the environment or culture. Treatment is focused on finding a single cause and using aggressive technological methods to attack the causal agent (Allan & Hall, 1988).

While this model has been useful in the treatment of infectious disease, it has been surprisingly ineffective at improving overall health. While mortality rates have improved, only 10% of this improvement can be attributed to medical intervention. All other improvements are the result of public health efforts, nutrition, and improved quality of life. In fact the 700% increase in health spending over the past 20 years has not produced any striking improvement in health. We are still significantly behind other developed nations in combating infant mortality, cancer deaths, and circulatory disease (Allan & Hall, 1988). As a result, critics are calling for the reallocation of funds toward a more holistic model of health promotion and disease prevention.

In addition to critiques of the medical model's efficacy, the model is also criticized for neglecting the human side of health and healing. While medicine focuses on the objective disease, it ignores the *illness*, which is the patient's subjective experience of the disease (Eisenberg, 1977). An attitude of "cure at all costs" (Watson, 1988b, p. 176), without addressing the problem of human suffering (Taylor & Watson, 1989) prevails.

In addition, the medical model has been criticized for taking control away from patients and for making normal life events—

such as childbirth, menopause, grief, and old age—medically managed and directed events. Finally, efforts to keep people alive are sometimes made without concern for the quality of these persons' lives (Allan & Hall, 1988). The recent popularity of the self-help suicide manual *Final Exit* attests to the public's disillusionment with these efforts and the desire to take back the control that has been handed over to modern medicine.

As an alternative to this medical model and the ethic that results from it, Gadow (1988) suggests that caring should be the overriding ethical framework of health care. Caring, according to Gadow, is the commitment to alleviate another's vulnerability. The exercise of power over another person, often with the use of expensive and invasive technological intervention, in an effort to cure disease, may increase rather than alleviate the vulnerability of the person. The case of Donald Cowart, a burn patient who was subjected to excruciatingly painful treatments in spite of his consistent refusal of treatment, is cited as an example of how overpowering a person, in the service of cure, can create a vulnerability "so extreme that no human caring can assuage it" (p. 8). Thus the activity of curing for its own sake is morally problematic and should be pursued only under the greater umbrella of caring.

Along with the limitations of the medical model and the ethical problems created by advanced technology, another problem—the rising cost of medical care—threatens to dehumanize the system even further. These exploding costs associated with the ever-expanding medical technology and the aging of the population have resulted in unprecedented efforts at cost containment. These efforts have focused on reducing the caregiver-to-client ratio rather than taking a critical look at the system itself. These cost-containment efforts are compounded by the fact that the intensities and severities of illness that are treated in the hospital are higher than they have ever been, and patients are being discharged sooner (Hull, 1985). As a result, hospital staff members are caring for sicker patients in a shorter period of time, with fewer resources.

Of serious concern is whether caring can even survive in this climate of cost containment and emphasis on technological quick fixes (Fry, 1988; Leininger, 1986). As Leininger points out, "the economic value of observing, comforting, and remaining with clients is receiving considerably less attention and less financial value compared with high technology in medical services" (p. 9).

To compound the problem further, a shortage of nursing and allied health professionals has plagued hospitals in recent years (Curtin, 1987; Jones, 1988). Some feel that this shortage is at least in part a result of the devaluing of care in the present health-care system. As Susan Reverby (1987) explains, "Unable to find a way to 'care with autonomy' and unable to separate caring from its valuing and basis, many nurses find themselves forced to abandon the effort to care, or nursing altogether" (p. 10).

As we have seen, the abandonment of care in the health-care system poses tremendous risks. No longer can we afford to separate mind from body and care from cure, or to emphasize the importance of one over the other. Increasing evidence over the past decade compels us to recognize the importance of the non-tangible aspects of healing (Achterberg, 1990).

The field of psychoneuroimmunology has established the links between feeling states and physiological responses, and it holds much promise for scientifically documenting the link between the experience of caring and feeling cared for and the physiological healing processes (Locke & Colligan, 1986; Pelletier & Herzing, 1989; Rossi, 1986). Achterberg (1990) explains this link:

> The aspects of healing associated with caring—hope, love, joy, expectation—are being documented as ingredients in the remission of disease. Second, negative forces such as loss of hope or love and the failure to adequately cope with stress have been identified as factors in both the onset and exacerbation of the symptoms of major illness. Even a decade ago, research was sketchy on these points. Now it extends through all fields of science and behavior. In short, the lack of caring or nurturing may be a primary causative factor in disease, and the "carers" are involved in directly facilitating cure. (pp. 192-193)

A frequently cited study by David McClelland (Ornstein & Sobel, 1987) illustrates this connection. He found that salivary immunoglobulin A concentrations, a measure of immune functioning, were increased in college students simply by watching a documentary of Mother Teresa of Calcutta caring for the sick. This suggests that even being in the presence of caring has a positive effect on the immune system.

A caring staff may affect the quality of services in other ways as well. Benner (1984), in an investigation of skill development in nursing, found that caring was an integral part of the development of skills and problem-solving abilities. Using the Dreyfus model of skill development, she explains that the most difficult problems to solve require perceptual ability as well as conceptual reasoning, and perceptual ability requires engagement and attentiveness. The intense involvement characteristic of caring allows for the perception of subtle cues that give rise to vague feelings and hunches characteristic of intuition (Benner, 1984). Thus technically competent caregivers who operate from a caring mode are able accurately to perceive subtle changes in the patient's condition before any objective criteria, such as vital sign changes, are evident. This expert level of practice is not possible without caring.

What Is Caring?

Essentially, caring is a way of being, a state of natural responsiveness to others. Because caring requires personal involvement, it is the antithesis of alienation, detachment, or apathy. One of the assumptions of this book is that caring is a natural condition of being human. This view is a departure from the traditional psychoanalytic understanding that humans are essentially self-serving creatures, driven by aggressive and unconscious forces that must be held in check by reaction formation, repression, and cultural reinforcement (Freud, 1961).

While self-serving aggression is a part of the human condition, we also have an innate responsiveness to the plight of others. How else can we explain the extraordinary behaviors of ordinary citizens who will put their lives in jeopardy to save the life of a stranger, or the mother who finds the strength to lift a car to free her child pinned beneath?

According to some anthropologists, this caring response is an integral part of our survival and one of the oldest and most universal attributes of human culture (Leininger, 1978). In fact, a natural instinct to care is necessary for our very survival and evolution, due to our inherent vulnerability as a species.

This vulnerability is created in part by our anatomical limitations. As humans evolved from walking on all fours to an upright position, the pelvis became thickened, and the birth canal subsequently narrowed. This anatomical change conflicted with our developing brain, which was becoming increasingly large. In order for the human fetus's head to fit through the cervical os, much of its brain growth and development had to occur after the time of birth, outside of the safety of the womb. This necessitated a period of prolonged helplessness and vulnerability that is unprecedented in other species (Ornstein & Sobel, 1987). Our very survival, then, depends upon our response to this vulnerability, and our most basic social structures are organized around the caring that is necessary for our continuation as a species.

Noddings (1984) theorizes that caring is based on our earliest experiences of being loved and protected and is a natural longing for this goodness. According to Noddings's theory, a morality of caring would be based on the natural experience of being cared for and the natural desire to be in a reciprocal caring relationship.

Caring, then, is a natural state of social involvement and responsiveness that is an integral part of our human condition. However, this natural state of responsiveness and commitment is not adequate by itself to ensure effective caring on a professional level. Clients who have contact with helping professionals expect more than good intentions. Therefore, helping professionals not only must be competent in the skills and science of their profession, but also must possess sophisticated relational and communication abilities to handle a variety of interpersonal and relational challenges and demands. In other words, making a commitment to care is not easy. Caregivers need to develop communication abilities that will allow them to continue to stay involved and continue to be therapeutic in the face of these demands and challenges. Otherwise, they may withdraw from a client out of frustration or a sense of powerlessness.

The Limitations of Psychological Models

Important developments in helping communication are represented by the humanistic tradition of understanding the helping relationship (Rogers, 1951) and the development of basic interviewing and nondirective communications skills. Guidelines such as those developed by Carkhuff (1969a, 1969b) and by Egan (1982) are recommended as a part of the reader's knowledge base. However, these concepts have limitations and are inadequate as a theory base for communication for health-care professionals.

First, these guidelines are more suited to a formal counseling situation than to the busy and often frantic health-care environment in which the client's intent is to receive a service rather than to develop a relationship, per se. As a result, health-care professionals may become frustrated by these expectations when their contacts with patients do not fit this model because they are too brief, or because patients are unwilling or unable to participate at this level.

Second, too much emphasis on communication techniques creates an additional problem. Caregivers complain that their communication seems contrived when speaking with patients in a therapeutic style, and rarely do they have the time to use reflective techniques that encourage elaboration of feelings; however, these basic interviewing skills remain the standard by which we teach and evaluate therapeutic communication. When the techniques themselves become the focus and are reified as a standard of good communication, they distance the caregiver from the subjective experience of being with the client and may interfere with genuine responsiveness. Furthermore, these techniques may be experienced by clients as patronizing.

Third, an additional concern is that skills and techniques do not teach caregivers about developing a relationship. In fact, techniques may reinforce distance if they are applied from a position of detached objectivity that is lacking in compassion. The concept of caring addresses this concern because it includes the personal and subjective involvement with the client, which is necessary for the appropriate integration and application of objective knowledge and skills.

So, while the client may not be seeking counseling, or a therapeutic relationship (and may be put off by attempts of health-care workers who make this assumption), the client, by the very fact that he or she requires human assistance, is in a position of vulnerability. Clients, then, need professionals who will be sensitive and responsive to this vulnerability, and who will facilitate their healing process.

Psychological models of counseling are inadequate to address this task. Helping clients to express and clarify their feelings may or may not be helpful. The complexity of the health-care environment demands a framework that will help clinicians to empower their clients whether they can actively participate in a relationship or are literally unconscious; whether their contacts are brief and intense, such as in an emergency room, or involve a long-term relationship, such as in a rehabilitation setting. Professionals need to be guided beyond technique, to respond in a way that is meaningful to each of their clients, and to negotiate the complexities of the caring relationship.

In the existing literature, very little is available to address this task. Caring is not a concept that is talked about in the communication literature, although it has been recognized that research in health communication must go beyond the medical model and must focus more on the relationship between the provider and the patient (Pettegrew & Logan, 1987).

Two

Theoretical Foundations of Caring

*T*he word *caring* has many meanings, and the concept has been studied from the perspectives of philosophy and nursing; however, caring has not been examined from a communication perspective. The first part of this chapter explores communication and related theories that have relevance for caring, and the next part reviews theories of caring from the perspectives of philosophy and nursing.

Communication Theories Related to Caring

The concept of caring communication has its roots in systems, relational, and dialectical traditions of communication. After reviewing the relational tradition, this section looks critically at confirmation and empathy, the constructs most commonly used to understand therapeutic or supportive communications. Next, the dialectical approach to relational communication is considered, and finally, some of the more recent developments in feminist psychology offer further understanding of the development of a caring relationship.

Relational Communication

The perspective of relational communication represents a shift away from studying the individual in a communication event to an analysis of the relationship (Millar & Rogers, 1976). At this level, relationships become ends in themselves, rather than merely a means to an end (Villard & Whipple, 1976, p. v). This is especially important in health care, for in health communication, "communication is the relationship" (Thompson, 1986, p. 6).

The relational model of communication developed out of the application of systems theory to human interaction (Millar & Rogers, 1976). Some of the early researchers contributing to relational theory are Bateson (1935, 1958), Haley (1963), Jackson (1959), Reusch (Reusch & Bateson, 1951), and Watzlawick, Beavin, and Jackson (1967).

One concept basic to an understanding of relational communication is the report and command aspects of communication. The *report aspect* refers to the content of the message, while the *command aspect* refers to how the message is to be taken, or ultimately to the relationship between the communicants (Reusch & Bateson, 1951). These two aspects are also referred to as the content and the relational components (Millar & Rogers, 1976). For example, an admissions clerk in a hospital may ask a patient for her insurance card. The *content* of the communication is clear; however, the clerk and this patient will also begin a process of communication that defines this patient's relationship with the hospital. The patient may feel cared for or dehumanized, depending on the *relational* component of the messages that are communicated between her and the staff members.

Watzlawick et al. (1967) hypothesized that the relationship aspects of communication are less evident in "healthy" relationships, while "sick" relationships "are characterized by a constant struggle about the nature of the relationship, with the content aspect of communication becoming less and less important" (p. 232). For example, communication with those patients labeled as "noncompliant" is dominated by relational messages (i.e., who is in control). As any caregiver knows, the content of the communication, which is the health care of the client, will be overshadowed by this struggle to determine who controls the treatment.

Another concept that arose from the relational tradition is the idea that behavior has no opposite; in other words, one cannot *not* behave. "If it is accepted that all behavior has message value, i.e., is communication, it follows that no matter how one may try, one cannot not communicate" (Watzlawick et al., 1967, pp. 48-49). This assumption is fundamental to the caring relationship, as all care-giving behaviors function as communication and, depending on the meaning created by the patient, will be interpreted as caring or as noncaring. For example, a nurse or technician might be carefully monitoring the patient's condition by checking intravenous lines, or other equipment, but if this caregiver did not look at or speak to the patient, the patient might perceive this behavior as uncaring.

Another widely adopted concept is that of *metacommunication*, the formal structure of communication. Metacommunication is a "communication about a communication" (Watzlawick et al., 1967, p. 53). It is the way in which we communicate about the relationship, similar to the command or relationship aspect of a communication. So, whenever we talk *about* a relationship, we are communicating at this level. Metacommunication also involves the implicit or explicit rules of human interaction that we often take for granted, but that become noticeable when they are broken in disturbed communication. For example, it is generally accepted that doctors and nurses can look at and touch patients' bodies quite freely, but what would happen if a patient touched a doctor or nurse in a similar fashion? Because this behavior violates the implicit rules of conduct in these situations, the professional would need to address the relationship by making these rules explicit.

Another concept of relational communication is that of analog-ical and digital communication (Watzlawick et al., 1967). While *digital communication* uses symbols, such as words, *analogical communication* is more concrete and represents objects by a likeness to that object. Nonverbal and more primitive attempts at communication are analogical. Human relationships use digital or symbolic communication to relate content and analogical communication to define the relational aspects; therefore, human relationships rely more on the analogical form of communication. For example, "I love you" is the digital form of communication, while physical attentiveness, embracing, and long soulful looks would be the analogical communication of love.

One could assume that within the context of providing care, much of the communication will be at the analogical level. With the possible exception of psychotherapy, the purpose of the caregiver-client relationship is to perform a service for the patient, not to communicate explicitly about the relationship. For a physical therapist to say "I care about you" is a less convincing expression of caring than for the therapist to spontaneously hug a patient who has just mastered the first independent steps following a stroke.

In summary, the relational tradition of communication focuses on the relationship rather than on the communication behaviors of the individuals, and it views the relationship as an end in itself. Relational communication tells us that messages have both a relational and a content dimension; that one cannot *not* communicate; that communication has a formal structure, that of meta-communication; and that communication occurs at an analogical as well as a digital level.

All of these concepts have become basic assumptions to any study of communication that focuses on the relationship created during the process of communication. Likewise, the concepts of confirmation and empathy contribute to our understanding of caring.

Confirmation

The concept of confirmation overlaps with caring. Like caring, confirmation has roots in a philosophical tradition. Buber (1957) described *confirmation* in this way:

> the measurement of humanness of a society. . . . The basis of man's life with man is twofold, and it is one—the wish of every man to be confirmed as what he is, even as what he can become, by men; and the innate capacity in man to confirm his fellow men in this way. . . . Actual humanity exists only where this capacity unfolds. (p. 102)

Laing (1961) defined confirmation as the "process through which individuals are recognized, acknowledged, and endorsed" (p. 83), he equated confirmation with love.

In order for an interaction to be called "confirming," four elements are necessary (Sieburg, 1973):

Recognition of the other's existence as an acting agent
Acknowledging the other's communication by responding to it relevantly
Congruence with and acceptance of the other's self-experience
Willingness on the part of the speaker to become involved with the other person

For example, Hanna, a patient suffering the mental deterioration that goes with Alzheimer's disease tried to grab hold of anyone passing by. While most of the staff tried to avoid Hanna, a nursing student was able to turn this uncomfortable situation into a confirming interaction. She recognized Hanna's existence as an acting agent, by assuming that her behavior was in some way purposeful, an expression of her feeling lost and frightened by the disorientation caused by her illness.

The student then acknowledged the behavior by responding to it relevantly. When the patient tried to grab hold of her, the student put her arm around Hanna, and invited her to walk with her. When they reached the end of the hallway, the student invited Hanna to sit in the lounge area. The student repeated this courtesy to Hanna whenever she walked by her, offering a momentary sense of acceptance and direction to offset Hanna's confusion. This action seemed congruent with Hanna's self-experience, as Hanna appeared more relaxed after each of these interactions. This student met the final criterion for a confirming interaction by her willingness to get involved with Hanna.

Confirmation is clearly related to caring. Maurice Friedman (1983) believes that "true confirmation is possible only in a caring society" and suggests Madeline Leininger's (1978, 1981) studies of caring across cultures as a context in which to understand confirmation. Thus there is considerable overlap between caring and confirmation. While confirmation is a part of caring, caring offers a broader framework, which may help in understanding at least two of Sieburg's elements: congruence with the other's self-perception and the willingness to be involved.

Empathy

Empathy is the communication concept that is commonly used to understand the professional's role in a helping or therapeutic relationship. Although empathy seems to be a necessary part of caring, conceptual problems may create confusion when empathy is applied with clients.

Empathy is commonly understood as an active imaginative understanding of another's feelings. In other words, health-care professionals must project themselves into their patient's world but then must be able to step back and analyze this experience based on their own experience and knowledge.

This view of empathy, which is inherited from psychological and counseling models, has been criticized in the communication literature for reinforcing a dualistic perspective. This is because empathy, as it is commonly understood, is rooted in our cultural values of individualism, which results in an artificial separation between the subject and object in communication or what Maurice Friedman (1974, as cited in Arnett & Nakagawa, 1983) calls the "psychologizing" of experience. He explains that this is the tendency to

> make the reality of our relationship to what is not ourselves—persons and cats, sunsets and trees—into what is essentially within ourselves. . . . The very notion of *having* experience . . . robs us of what experience once meant—something which can take us up, take us outside ourselves and bring us into relationship with the surprising, the unique, the other. (p. 372; emphasis in original)

Friedman (1974) relates an incident about Martin Buber, which contrasts the difference between the "psychologistic" impulse to own an experience and the willingness to participate fully in a dialogue. As Buber was speaking in a lecture-discussion format, he mentioned that he wished people would ask more questions. His view was not that he owned or possessed knowledge but that when someone comes to him with a question the wisdom "happens, comes to be in the *between*" (p. 372).

Thus an understanding of empathy that is based on our cultural values of individualism and of owning or possessing experience may remove the listener from a true appreciation of the experience with another. As a result, in the communication field, there has been a call for a broader framework (Broome, 1985; Gordon, 1985). Gordon (1985), for example, suggests Mayeroff's (1971) work on caring as a possible framework (Mayeroff's theory is presented later in this chapter).

The following vignette further illustrates the limitations of a traditional view of empathy to explain the process of interpersonal knowing: A nurse was caring for a man who was extremely anxious about having to face emergency open-heart surgery. He had always lived a healthy and active life, and the seriousness of his cardiac problem was quite a shock to him. He was feeling panic stricken and did not believe he could go through with the surgery. The nurse tried to calm him down. At one point, he said with great intensity, "I'm just no hero, I just can't go through with this!" This nurse responded by saying forcefully, "Heros are ordinary people faced with extraordinary circumstances, and instead of running away, they stand and face whatever the circumstance is!" This hit him like a "cold washcloth to the face," and he said "Where did you hear that?" The nurse was somewhat embarrassed and told him that she had just made it up. He repeated her statement often and credited her with getting him through the experience. He did well with his surgery and recovery and was out of the hospital quickly. To this day, he visits the unit every year to bring a gift of flowers or candy for the nurses and to give special thanks to the nurse who helped him through the experience.

When questioned about her response, this nurse did not recall ever having felt as this man did, or ever being in a similar situation that might allow her to identify with him. Her understanding did not involve active projection or putting herself in his position. She didn't need to distance herself in order to objectively analyze the situation to know what to do. In fact, her understanding of what she said did not seem to be experienced at a conceptual level. She had no idea where her idea came from. This is an example of understanding that is characterized by receptivity. She allowed herself on some level to become one with his experience and subliminally received from him what he desperately needed to hear. It was as though her consciousness acted as a conductor to provide the completion of his idea, in the way an electric current will occur if it has a medium to complete its circuit (Montgomery, 1991a, 1991b, 1992).

The preceding example illustrates that communication does not occur from a position of interpersonal distance or within a fixed self-boundary. Communication, as it is commonly depicted, shows messages being sent back and forth as arrows between two separate and discrete entities—sender, and receiver, as shown in Figure 2.1.

In contrast, the ideas of empathy and caring challenge the assumption that we communicate from a position of distance and from within discrete boundaries. As empathy is traditionally understood from the psychoanalytic perspective, one must merge with or incorporate the other person's subjective experience in

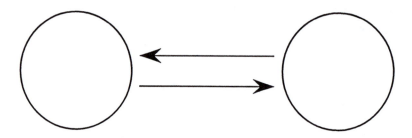

Figure 2.1. Sender-Receiver View of Communication

order to feel what he or she feels. From this perspective, communication during an empathic encounter would look more like two circles that overlap to some degree, as shown in Figure 2.2.

Nevertheless, the psychoanalytic perspective presents us with a paradox because, while therapists are expected to merge in this way, they must simultaneously be able to detach from the other person's subjective perspective and maintain enough distance so that the therapist's objectivity is not threatened. The term *detached concern* is sometimes used to describe an appropriate amount of closeness/distance (Lief & Fox, 1963; Miller, Stiff, & Ellis, 1988; Wilson & Kneisel, 1988) by health-care workers.

This paradox creates confusion when it is applied to clinical practice. For example, Flaskerud, Halloran, Janken, Lund, and Zetterlund (1979) believe that the concept of empathy sets a tone for distance in the nurse-patient relationship. These authors conducted a descrip-

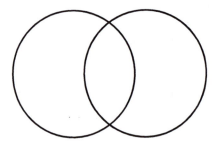

Figure 2.2. Merger That Occurs During Empathy

tive study of nursing in the naturalistic environment and found that the nurse-patient relationship was characterized by avoidance and distance. They suggest that the message in nursing education, to be close to patients but not too close, is based on empathy:

> The nurse achieves an understanding of the patient through both sympathy and empathy, yet empathy is different from sympathy in that a certain amount of distance is maintained to allow for objectivity. Thus, the nurse-patient relationship is built upon the concept of distance. Unfortunately the appropriate amount of distance has never been defined. (p. 170)

The use of the term *boundaries*, generally used to describe the appropriate amount of interpersonal distance between therapists and clients, adds to this confusion. Generally, the phrase "appropriate boundaries" is used to admonish caregivers from getting "too involved" (Pasacreta & Jacobsen, 1989; Stiver, 1991); yet the nature of an appropriate boundary has yet to be specified. Maslach (1983) recommends adopting the other's perspective rather than feeling the other person's emotions as one way to maintain this separation, but separating emotional from intellectual empathy is impossible in the realities of caregiving (Munley, 1985).

Thus a contradiction seems to exist between the need for immersion and the need for interpersonal distance in the helping relationship. Several more recent perspectives transcend these contradictions. One is that of nursing theorist Martha Rogers. While it is beyond the scope of this chapter to present her entire theory, Wheeler (1988) has applied this theory to the concept of empathy. According to Rogers (1970), human beings are energy fields, distinguished by patterns rather than discrete boundaries. Empathy, according to Wheeler, can be understood as the interaction of these human energy fields. Each individual's field has a unique pattern but is integral with other fields. During empathy, the caregiver's field is shared with the client's, and vice versa. While interacting, these energy fields move toward increasing differentiation and complexity (growth). Thus the merger of these fields stimulates self-differentiation; and conversely the more self-differentiation, the more the caregiver is able to experience this union. Empathy, the pattern that emerges from this interaction, is a shared single rhythm where formerly two rhythms existed.

The Dialectical Approach to Relational Communication

Another perspective that transcends the contradictions involved in empathy is dialectical theory. A dialectical formulation views the contradictions of closeness/distance as essential to the development of close interpersonal bonds (Rawlins, 1983).

Altman, Vinsel, and Brown (1981) identify three features of dialectical thinking that are relevant to human behavior: "(1) the idea of opposites or polarity, (2) the unity of opposites, and (3) the dynamic relationship between opposites" (p. 118). The idea of opposition or contradiction, essential to any discussion of dialectics, is represented in many areas of thought, including the Chinese philosophy of yin and yang, Freud's id and superego, and Jung's animus and anima (Altman et al., 1981). The merger-separateness polarity described in empathy then cannot be addressed as independent entities, but must be viewed within a unified framework, as these opposites are merely opposite ends of a unified whole.

The idea of the unity of opposites includes the complementarity and integration of opposites, and the relative strength and balance of opposites. Complementarity implies that each pole provides a definitional base for the other. The strength and balance of opposites assumes that no pole completely dominates or contradicts the other. On the other hand, the notion of homeostasis or equilibrium is not necessarily the ideal relationship between the two poles. "The relationship between opposites can assume any of a series of relative strengths (excluding 100:0 or 0:100), and none is inherently better than any other" (Altman et al., 1981). There then would be no predetermined best ratio of union and separation involved in empathy.

Finally, the dynamic relationship between opposites deals with change. Altman et al. (1981) suggest a view of change that is different from Hegel's idea of some ultimate synthesis of opposites that would lead to an ideal state. Instead, in relational communication, flexible adaptation to dialectical tensions is viewed as the ideal. According to Baxter (1988), change itself is caused by the very struggle and tension of contradiction. Perhaps this tension is one of the factors in the therapeutic relationship that facilitates change in the client.

Baxter (1989) suggests that the presence of paired opposites is necessary for change and growth to occur. One of these paired opposites is autonomy-connection:

No relationship can exist unless the parties forsake individual autonomy. However, too much connection paradoxically destroys the relationship because the individual entities become lost. Simultaneously,
autonomy can be conceptualized only in terms of separation from
others. But too much autonomy paradoxically destroys the individual's
identity, because connections with others are necessary to identity
formation and maintenance. (p. 3)

Thus from this perspective, the paradox and contradiction of
giving up one's separateness to merge with another, while not
losing oneself, is an ongoing tension of intimate relationships.

Feminist Theorists

Feminist psychology provides further insights into the issues of
relational communication. Judith Jordan (1989), Carol Gilligan
(1982), Jean Baker Miller (1976), Nancy Chodorow (1978), Belenky
et al. (1986), and others point out that our understanding of
relationships is limited by existing theories of human development because they overemphasize issues of autonomy and other
values that are more reflective of the masculine experience in our
culture.

According to Gilligan (1982), male and female experiences represent different human truths, "the former of the role of separation
as it defines and empowers the self, the latter of the ongoing
process of attachment that creates and sustains the human community" (p. 156). While male psychological growth has been characterized as developing autonomy by establishing increasing distance from the primary love object (mother), females develop a
sense of self through identification with the mother, thus their
psychology is characterized by relationships and attachments.
The importance of attachments, however, is minimized in linear
formulations of the life cycle that reduce development to increasing separation and independence. As a result of these assumptions, the basic human needs for dependency and deep relational
involvements have been infantilized and pathologized (Jordan,
1989).

Judith Jordan (1989) talks about the individualistic assumptions
on which most theories of relationships and human development
are based:

The spatial metaphor of the real me buried deep inside the body makes it seem that the real self is only impinged upon and damaged by relationships. This leads to conceiving boundaries as a wall, protecting intrapsychic reality from external influence.

Empathy, according to Jordan, is a deep appreciation of the unique qualities of a particular person—that by "moving more fully into the particular, we can experience the universal." What is missing from most models of empathy is the sense of commonality, joining, mutuality, and increased sense of relatedness. We not only recognize the self in the other, but we also recognize the other in ourselves. This need for connection and emotional joining is the primary need met by empathy.

A feminist view also offers a different perspective of our sense of responsibility in relationships. Gilligan (1982) studied the development of moral reasoning in women and found that development was characterized by a movement from survival to traditional notions of goodness and self-sacrifice, and finally to "a reflective understanding of care as the most adequate guide to the resolution of conflicts in human relationships" (p. 105). This understanding is the natural outcome of the realization that all of us are essentially interconnected and interdependent. The activity of care then, becomes not just a desire to please and to help others, but a form of expression that enhances both ourselves and those for whom we care.

Noddings (1984) developed a relational ethic of caring based on the feminine values of receptivity, relatedness, and responsiveness. According to Noddings, caring is a "longing for goodness" (p. 2); it is a way to meet the other morally that is based on our earliest memories of being cared for. Noddings (1984), questioning the ontological assumptions that define empathy, comments on the *Oxford University Dictionary's* definition of empathy as: "the power of projecting one's personality into, and so fully understanding the object of contemplation" (p. 30). Noddings describes this as a "peculiarly rational, western, masculine way of looking at 'feeling with'" (p. 30). Her view of empathy is receptive rather projective. "I receive the other into myself, and I see and feel with the other. I become a duality" (p. 30).

The way in which women conceptualize their world may also affect the way in which they communicate at the relational level.

Belenky et al. (1986) studied the way women think and learn in ways that are different from men. The traditional educational system is based on abstract critical thought, the development of autonomy and independence, and a morality of rights and justice. Women, on the other hand, are more apt to think in terms of interdependence, intimacy, nurturance, and contextual thought.

These so-called feminine ways of thinking have been characterized as emotional thoughts that interfere with intellectual reasoning. Thus women may feel alienated from what are represented as abstract intellectual truths. As some women grow in their cognitive development, Belenky et al. found that their thinking contrasted from the "separate knowing" that characterized men, to a "connected" way of understanding that is based on contextual understanding and an integration of caring into their work. Because the medical environment is dominated by masculine models of thinking and reasoning, those who care, and consequently become immersed in integrated and contextual understandings, whether they be men or women, often feel alienated and may find their concerns trivialized or ignored.

This review of the feminist perspective suggests that caring cannot be understood within traditional psychological views of relationships that emphasize distance and objectivity. Caring professionals, both men and women, educated within this traditional view are apt to dismiss their subjective concerns about patients as trivial or inappropriate, and they may feel the need to keep a safe emotional distance from patients. Theories grounded in the feminine experience, on the other hand, validate a natural desire to immerse oneself in the concerns of others.

Summary of Caring in Relation to Existing Theories

Systems and relational traditions of communication have changed the focus from the individual in a communication event to the relationship that is created between the two parties. Distinguishing the relational from the content aspect of the message, and distinguishing communication from communication about the communication (metacommunication), allows exploration of the more complex dimensions of human communication.

Empathy and confirmation, the constructs generally used to understand helping communication, are components of caring but are not sufficient to capture the complexity of caring. In addition, problems with the concept of empathy create confusion at the clinical level and may reinforce the adopting of a position of distance and objectivity when working with clients. Relational dialectics provides a unifying framework for understanding the paradox of union and distance that is inherent to the concept of empathy. Finally, a feminist perspective of relationships validates the concerns for context, subjectivity, and connectedness that are integral to a caring response.

Theories of Caring

Theories of caring have been developed in the fields of nursing and philosophy. Although there is a fairly large body of literature on caring, only those theories most relevant to the communication aspect of caring are addressed here.

Mayeroff's Theory of Caring

Perhaps the first person to address comprehensively the concept of a caring relationship was Milton Mayeroff, a philosopher, who in 1971 wrote a brief but elegant book, *On Caring*. Mayeroff saw caring as an existential position that provides order and meaning to life, the basis on which we organize our involvements and feel our place in the world. Thus caring is not limited to interpersonal relationships. According to Mayeroff, one can care deeply for and organize one's life around an idea, a philosophical ideal, or a community. The major ingredients of caring, according to Mayeroff, are as follows:

Knowing—Caring requires knowledge of the other. One must be able to understand the other's needs and respond properly to them. Good intentions alone do not guarantee a caring response.

Alternating Rhythms—One learns from one's mistakes and modifies behavior in response to the other. Another important form of rhythm is that of moving back and forth between a narrower and a wider framework, so one can go from attending to detail to attending to the larger context.

Patience—One must have the patience to allow another to grow "in its own time and in its own way." We not only give the other time, but we also give space, by giving the other "room to live" (p. 13).

Honesty—Honesty involves being open to oneself as well as to the other. The one who is caring must be honest enough to accept the other as he or she actually is rather than how the caring one would like him or her to be.

Trust—Trust requires faith in the ability of the other to grow and self-actualize in that person's own time and way. "It appreciates the independent existence of the other, that the other is *other*. . . . Trusting the other is to let go; it includes an element of risk and a leap into the unknown, both of which take courage" (pp. 14-15; emphasis in original).

Humility—Humility involves being willing to learn from the one being cared for. This requires overcoming the arrogance that exaggerates the power of the one who is caring, at the expense of the one being cared for.

Hope—The hope is that the other will grow through caring. This hope is not based on the hope of an idealized future at the expense of the present, but rather "an expression of . . . a present alive with a sense of the possible" (p. 19).

Courage—Courage is required in order to follow the lead of the other into the unknown. This is similar to the courage of the artist who rejects conformity in order to create independently and in so doing comes to find personal expression.

Mayeroff thus provides a descriptive overview of the qualities necessary for caring. His work, while it does not address itself specifically to clinical practice, captures the essential nature of caring from a philosophical perspective.

Jean Watson's Theory of Caring in Nursing

Jean Watson (1985, 1988a) has developed caring as a theory of nursing. Her theory draws from the works of existential humanistic psychology and philosophy, as well as from recent advances in physical science and neuroscience. Watson's theory incorporates a metaphysical dimension that is especially relevant to the discussion of the union that occurs between the caregiver and the client and the nature of interpersonal knowing that we call "empathy."

According to Watson (1989), caring is a transpersonal, intersubjective, mutual exchange between the nurse and the client. She describes this intersubjectivity in this way:

> An ideal of intersubjectivity and transcendence is based upon a belief that people learn from each other how to be human by finding their dilemmas in themselves. What is learned from others is self-knowledge. The self learned about or discovered is every self; it is universal, the human self. People learn to recognize themselves in others. The intersubjectivity keeps alive a common humanity. (p. 180)

In other words, both the client and the caregiver relate at the level of their own humanness and vulnerability, and they learn from each other. This shared humanity allows them to transcend themselves by feeling a part of something greater than themselves.

Watson takes this transcendence further by incorporating the idea of spirit. A caring occasion incorporates the gist or spirit of both patient and nurse, and an actual union occurs in which the phenomenological fields of both merge to become one. In becoming one, they become part of something greater. According to Watson (1985),

> In a transpersonal caring relationship, a spiritual union occurs between the two persons, where both are capable of transcending self, time, space, and the life history of the other. In other words, the nurse enters into the experience (phenomenal field) of another and the other person enters into the nurse's experience. This shared experience creates its own phenomenal field and becomes part of a larger, deeper, complex pattern of life. (pp. 66-67)

Thus caring provides access to a greater force—a primal and universal psychic energy, similar to love. This energy creates a sense of harmony of mind, body, and spirit, which can actually potentiate the self-healing process. Although Watson originally drew these ideas from the works of philosophers such as Whitehead (1953) and de Chardin (1967), recently, she has drawn support for these ideas from the holographic paradigm of science, based on the work of Battista (1982), Harman (1982, 1987a, 1987b), Pribram (1971), and Wilber (1982). These ideas posit that consciousness exists as an energy field beyond the limits of space and time, supporting the idea that a caring consciousness does in fact transcend the limits of space and time and can in fact create its own healing.

Many clinicians can recall moments of total immersion with a patient, during which they lost track of time and later felt that something special or magical had occurred. These "caring moments," as Watson calls them, are often a turning point in the patient's recovery or response to treatment.

In summary, according to Watson's theory, caring is a mutual exchange in which both parties relate on the level of their shared humanness, and both learn from each other. This equality is strikingly different from the professional distance that many caregivers are advised to maintain. The nurse and the patient experience a union at the level of spirit, giving them access to a greater energy that serves as a source of self-renewal and healing. By incorporating the idea of spirit, Watson brings to light the invisible aspects of caring communication and explains the power of these moments.

Gendron's Analysis of the Expressive Form of Caring Communication

As we can see from the previous theories, the communication of caring transcends technique. Its expression arises from each context as a unique and creative process. Diane Gendron (1988) addresses this creative quality by analyzing caring communication as an aesthetic form. According to Gendron, caring cannot be understood in terms of isolated communication behaviors, but as "the total form or gestalt of what the patient perceives" (p. 30). She identifies four elements of this form: expressive form, channels of communication, dynamic sensorimotor responses, and the metaphor of orchestral music.

Expressive Form

According to Langer (1967), human feelings have certain forms that are conveyed symbolically through art. These forms include such elements as tone, rhythm, balance, harmony, unity, and both the tension and resolution of tension that is characteristic of many art forms. These elements are also present during the communication of caring. Gendron also draws on neuropsychological research that has identified "essentic forms" (Clynes, 1979) of emotion,

elemental units within the nervous system, which are programmed
to recognize and produce certain emotions. Thus if caring is an
emotion, it has a certain organismic pattern that will be felt and
recognized automatically by the patient at a neurological level.

Channels of Communication

Caring is communicated through both verbal and nonverbal
channels of communication. Nonverbal channels communicate
the relational components of the message. An estimated 55% to
70% of feeling is communicated through nonverbal channels (Argyle, 1979; Birdwhistell, 1970), including physical appearance and
dress (organismics), eye movements (oculesics), the way space is
used (proxemics), the way time is used (chronemics), touch (haptics),
body movement (kinesics), voice (vocalics and paralinguistics), and
the way the objects are used (objectics) (Egolf & Chester, 1976).

Dynamic Sensorimotor Responses

Dynamic sensorimotor responses are based on the work of
Werner and Kaplan (1963), who studied affective sensorimotor
patterns during infancy. They found that "objects are given structure, form, and meaning by an organismic integration of sensory,
affective, imaginative, and postural experiences" (Gendron, 1988,
p. 8). This integration allows for symbol formation and a transcendence beyond the comprehension of the mere sensory elements to
a more organismic understanding, so that one can understand "a
harsh color," or "a sweet sound" (Gendron, 1988, p. 9). Thus when
a health-care professional interacts with a patient, the patient will
experience an integration of the affective sensorimotor patterns,
such that the professional's physical ministrations may be interpreted as gentle or harsh.

Metaphor of Orchestral Music

The metaphor of orchestral music is used to capture themes that
are present across all the different channels of communication (Gendron, 1988). This metaphor includes general themes of polarity, temperature, force, texture-shape, and directionality. These themes then
interact within the dimensions of harmony and melody.

The first theme, *polarity*, is positive rather than negative and is expressed through behaviors such as humor, mobilizing hope, and promoting growth. *Temperature* is expressed as warmth, which is communicated through nonverbal behaviors, such as smiling, friendliness, and humor. The *force* is gentle and may be expressed through eye contact and calm, unhurried actions. *Texture-shape* is characterized as smooth and soft, as opposed to rough and harsh; and as being curved, as opposed to angular. The elements of texture-shape are communicated by paralinguistics, facial expressions, gestures, and the ways that time and space are used during the communication (Gendron, 1988). *Directionality* is toward the other, open and giving; this is evidenced by physical movements that reflect attention, such as eye contact, attending behaviors, and concrete tasks done for the patient.

The dimension of *harmony* describes how the caregiver's behavior within these themes proceeds as "a flowing matrix" over time (Gendron, 1988, p. 14). This involves congruence of themes across channels, and matching of the caregiver's response with the patient's perspective. The melody dimension includes the concept of rhythm. Regular and synchronous rhythm is consistent with the studies of Condon (1979) and Kendon (1979), in which they discovered the synchronization of babies' movements to the movements of adults in the room; they called this "entrainment." In addition, Gendron cites Chapple's (1970) work, in which he found that synchronous communication is related to feelings of well-being:

> Synchronous interaction promotes emotions of well-being and affection via the limbic system, hypothalamus and autonomic nervous system whereas asynchronous interaction induces stress and behaviors such as withdrawal and impatience. (as quoted in Gendron, 1988, p. 24)

In summary, Gendron goes beyond the view of caring as an isolated set of communication behaviors. By incorporating neuropsychological research within an aesthetic framework, she describes caring's essential organismic form. This form involves a highly complex synchronization and organismic integration of subtle verbal and nonverbal cues that all come together in a way that could be compared to a well-orchestrated symphony.

Gaut's Analysis

Finally, Gaut provides an analysis of caring and defines the necessary and sufficient conditions for caring within the health-care context. Based on a semantic and philosophical analysis, Gaut (1983) identified three general meanings associated with caring: (a) attention and concern, (b) "responsibility for or providing for" (p. 315), and (c) "regard, fondness, or attachment" (p. 315).

Gaut (1983) also has identified the necessary and sufficient conditions that define a caring act: (a) There must be an awareness of the need for care; (b) the caregiver must have knowledge of how to improve the situation; (c) the caregiver must have the intention to help; (d) an action must be chosen and implemented; and (e) the change in the client must be based on what is good for that client, rather than some other person or conditions.

This analysis further describes caring by including the conditions of knowledge and action. Supportive or empathic communication alone is not adequate for caring to occur. This view is supported by research indicating that patients recognize caring as clinical competence (Brown, 1986; Cronin & Harrison, 1988; Larson, 1984; Mayer, 1987).

Summary of Caring as a Communication Phenomenon

Caring, as described in this section of this text, is a highly complex communication phenomenon that occurs at the level of biology, behavior, and metaphysics. The qualities necessary for caring, according to Mayeroff, are knowing, alternating rhythms, patience, honesty, trust, humility, hope, and courage. According to Watson, the caregiver and client experience a union that allows them access to a greater force or consciousness, that transcends time and space and is a source of healing and self-renewal. The caring relationship is mutual and intersubjective, as both parties fully enter the relationship and experience growth.

According to Gendron, the client recognizes caring, not as isolated communication behaviors, but as a gestalt form. The recognition of this form involves a highly complex synchronization and integration of subtle verbal and nonverbal cues. The overall effect has an aesthetic quality and can be compared to orchestral music.

Finally, Gaut points out that this communication and the relationship itself is not complete without necessary knowledge and action on behalf of the one being cared for. This is particularly important in health care, for the action itself is the focus of health care and is what the patient may identify as the expression of caring.

Part II

The Theory of Caring

Three

Caring Begins With the Caregiver

Predispositional Qualities of the Caregiver

*A*lthough caring, as described in Chapter 2, is characterized by a great deal of mutuality between caregiver and client, the caregiver has a certain predisposition, an existential way of being in relation to others, that allows for and sustains this level of communication. This predisposition includes seven qualities: (a) person orientation rather than role orientation, (b) concern for the human element in health care, (c) person-centered intention, (d) transcendence of judgment, (e) hopeful orientation, (f) lack of ego involvement, and (g) expanded personal boundaries.

Person Orientation Versus Role Orientation

The position of the caregiver as he or she encounters a patient is characterized by a willingness to give and share on a more intimate personal level rather than from a professional persona. As one occupational therapist explains, "it's hard to separate your personal from your professional [self] because the values . . . the inner parts of me are the same." A medical-surgical nurse further explains, "it doesn't involve me as a person beyond being a professional until I am able to interact with a person in such a way that their honesty about them as a person and my honesty about me as a person [come] out. . . . That's when you get to the real caring." Stepping out of role is somewhat of a paradox because as another nurse says, "when you step out of that [professional role] is when you embrace it the most. . . . This is the part you always try and push away before you understand it."

To illustrate, a psychiatric nurse shared an experience in which she stepped out of role and allowed her humanness to become engaged with a patient. She was coleading a goals group with hospitalized psychiatric patients, which she described as usually being very routine and somewhat boring. As they went around the room and asked patients to identify their goals for the week, they came to a patient who was very suicidal. In fact, the nurse felt that, unless something drastic happened, he would probably leave the hospital and kill himself:

> When we got to him, he said "well, I don't have any goals for this week." That was not at all unusual . . . and usually we go, "well fine, if later on, some come to you, you are assigned to so and so, and you can talk to them." But unlike how I usually reacted to that kind of resistance, which was "fine, if that's where you are at, that's where you are," we did in fact move on to the next person, but what I started experiencing was not just sadness, but I felt like putting my head on my hands and bawling my eyes out. I felt like sobbing.

She tried to sort out and understand her feelings and realized her reaction was very connected to what was going on, not just with the suicidal patient, Bob,[1] but with other members of the group as well. (How she came to this conclusion is described further in Chapter 4, in regard to "use of self"):

> I turned and I looked at Bob, and tears came to my eyes and I said "You know, Bob, I feel like I'm losing you, and I don't know what to do." He was just incredibly armored and distancing, and . . . his whole body countenance changed and light came into his eyes and tears came into his eyes, and he kind of clutched his chest and said, "God, I can't tell you how much this means to me."

This incident became a critical turning point in this patient's therapy.

What this nurse did in this group was very different from her role-driven behavior prior to the group. She described that she was perhaps going overboard in providing structure and keeping things safe, perhaps, "being too professional":

> Well, I think in a lot of ways my role on that team was to provide a lot of structure, and I think sometimes I could go overboard with, with keeping things safe. . . . I think that we were so freaked out by the fact that people were trying to kill themselves on the unit. . . . I don't think we were being human about our own fears and concerns about what the patients were doing.

While providing structure and keeping things safe was an important part of her role, stepping out from behind this role and allowing herself to be human and to be touched by this man's despair imparted a healing power to the communication.

Concern for the Human Element of Health Care

Successful caregivers possess a philosophical view that recognizes the wholeness and integrity of that which is human and of the fragility of this human factor in the technological environment of health care. The following is a description of how one nurse views her role in the highly technical environment of the operating room:

> I kind of look for horror in the face of a first time student. I want to see them be a little overwhelmed by the blood and the smell and the whole experience, you know. This body that appears to be lifeless that is only asleep, but you know they are just totally vulnerable. Totally vulnerable, and that you as the nurse in the room are really the person to make sure that vulnerability is never lost sight of because even though the surgeon is operating and the anesthesiologist is keeping the patient asleep, you are the one who is responsible for their whole human integrity remaining intact.

A medical surgical nurse described the pressure on a medical surgical unit to do more and more tasks and how that tends to create an atmosphere of dehumanization of patients:

You can objectify them [patients] because they become this need, this demand on your time, this thing you have to do. It's not like a person but all the things around them that you have to do for them, so instead you dehumanize them. . . . On the other hand, when I get involved with someone in a caring relationship, I know that person and . . . I don't dehumanize . . . them, separate their need from them.

The ability to see the wholeness and vulnerability of the person allows caregivers to see beyond the specific focus of their discipline or the specific problem that they are treating. An occupational therapist has learned to "think globally" about each patient situation. A speech pathologist illustrates the healing that can occur when caregivers are sensitive to and respond to the humanness of the situation. This speech pathologist was working with a 4-year-old child who had no speech at all. She was supposed to be doing speech drills with him to help him develop his language abilities.

I'll never forget this child. . . . I can remember taking him into the classroom, he'd just scream and scream, he was just so upset. And I finally just picked him up and sat down in the rocking chair and just started singing to him and rocking him because it just seemed like he was so scared or so frustrated. I didn't know what was wrong with him, but he just seemed like he needed some of that. And I started singing some familiar songs, and all of a sudden he tried to sing with me. It was the first time we had heard anything from him that was intentional. Something went on there, and I'm not sure what it was.

Person-Centered Intention

As the preceding example illustrates, caring is motivated principally by the intention to connect with the client in a way that is helpful. This intention is different from helping that is driven by a depersonalized agenda for the client, such as performing a task or curing a disease. While the expertise that the clinician has to offer certainly does suggest an agenda, this is the curing part of the role.

Caring clinicians, however, apply their curative skills within a caring relationship. The caring relationship has no agenda other than to connect with the client. As one occupational therapist explains, "The feeling of engagement is more important than the technical aspect." As the preceding example showed, the speech therapist was able to put aside her technical agenda of doing speech drills so that she could connect with this child. In order to keep the client ahead of the professional agenda, as one nurse says, "You have to let go of your own expectations of the client."

A dying child helped an occupational therapist learn this lesson. While her agenda was to teach him developmental skills, she was able to keep this agenda in perspective. She explains, "Tomorrow, if someone calls me and tells me that child died, I wouldn't be as concerned that he learned to feed himself . . . , but that I knew that he knew that I loved him."

When caregivers relate from the intention to connect with rather than to do to a person, the communication can have a healing effect. A psychiatric nurse recalls her experience in working with a patient with Alzheimer's disease, in which she described being able to transmit her positive intention without words:

> He was at that stage of the illness where he knew that something was missing and he was very very disorganized. And he was very frightened and I just, I just stood behind him kind of like this you know [*demonstrated putting hands on shoulders*] with my hands on him and just kind of grounded him, and the way he interpreted that was "this is kind, these people are kind, this place is kind."

She explains:

> you don't even have to say all the right things or be all the right things or do all the right things. My intention is to be helpful and be connected. I can . . . make lots of mistakes as far as theory goes and that patient will pick up on that intention.

Transcending Judgment

While all health-care professionals are expected to be nonjudgmental, this expectation can be difficult when they are faced with clients who challenge their values or are just difficult to like. While most caregivers recognize that they just can't work with some people, caring professionals have an expanded repertoire of people whom they are able to accept and care about. In order to do this, they have to develop some sort of philosophical or spiritual understanding that enables them to tolerate and accept a wide variety of human experience.

An operating room nurse explained how enriching it has been for her to go outside of the limits of her own life:

> People have requirements for who they involve in their life. You know they have to . . . be tall, gorgeous, blond, free of social disease. . . . I mean we categorize the people we want to spend our lives with and we don't like to go outside of those categories because they are threatening or they are not nice . . . and at the same time when we do that we limit the opportunity to experience a thousand different life times through someone else's eyes who may not fit into those nice organized little categories.

She went on to describe a situation where a prisoner was brought into the operating room accompanied by the police. He was unconscious and in leg irons. She made the police remove the leg irons and leave the operating room:

> I mean the guy was a rapist and a murderer . . . the worst kind of human being that [anyone] could imagine, but he was a dying human being. . . . I honestly don't believe we are there to judge, nor do we of all people have the right. We are in a profession that is supposed to soar above those things, and if you can't soar above them, then you are in the wrong business.

For some, this view of human nature is learned from experience. One nurse has learned this after working for years in an ICU of a public hospital:

> You're going to meet some horrible people who are going nowhere, but for the most part, you give everybody a chance and they're going to give you something back to prove you wrong. Everybody's got something nice about them. Sometimes you have to dig.

Expert caregivers learn that judgments are simply not meaningful, as they interfere with caring. An occupational therapist was trying to work with a child with cerebral palsy who would "just scream and bite, and just be impossible. And I held him without any sense of anger, and just let him be, and tried to convey that I could honor [that] whatever he needed to feel, he needed to feel. And his screams lessened, and I just held him."

A social worker who works with children and families has an understanding that allows him to care about even the most destructive parents. He explains, "Even the most abusive parents are trying to do the best they can with what they have. The problem is that they don't have the skills they need. I approach it from that angle."

While value judgments about clients are usually based on abstract principles of what someone believes is right or wrong, in caring, the relationship is what is right, and this takes precedence over abstract moral principles. This commitment to the relationship makes it possible for the caregiver to stay involved with and be accepting of clients who might not share the same values or make similar choices. A psychiatrist explains: "The relationship is what's right. . . . Whoever you're with, you're with, and wherever they are is where you need to be, and then you look at how that works for them. . . . This may make one feel like a chameleon sometimes, but it's extremely helpful because it allows us to get with people . . . and not be judgmental."

Of course, knowledge and education also help to dispel the misunderstandings that may lead to judgments. The aforementioned psychiatrist works with developmentally disabled individuals. She was worried about one of her patients because he keeps himself decorated in swastikas and other racist insignias. "The first pass glance at this guy, if you ran into him in a shopping center would be 'oh, my God!'" but she is able to see beyond this because her knowledge of his cognitive functioning lets her know that he does not have the intellectual ability to understand the symbolic significance of these insignias. "If you talk to him, he's a teddy bear . . . [the presence of these insignias] does not relate to what the inner person is about."

Hopeful Orientation

In order to stay involved with people who are in the worst of circumstances, caregivers need to be able to find positive meaning, possibilities, and hope in situations that may appear bleak at best. A positive, hopeful orientation gives caregivers the courage to get involved and sustains them during their involvement. A sense of possibility also enables the caregiver to act as a resource for patients who cannot see beyond their despair.

These caring professionals tend to be very connected with others, so they are able to draw strength and meaning from a variety of sources. One of the most significant sources of inspiration for caregivers, which is discussed in Chapter 10, is the patients themselves. In addition, confidence in the skills of their discipline, a supportive team, and a fulfilling personal life are other sources from which they derive meaning, which allows for a general sense of optimism and hope.

An optimistic outlook is not only helpful, but even critical in some situations. A rehabilitation nurse described how she felt when a patient, a young woman with a brain stem stroke, was transferred to her unit. This patient was described as a "vegetable." The prognosis given by the physicians was very bleak. She was sent to the rehabilitation unit because they didn't know what else to do.

When the nurse first saw her, her reaction was, "Oh my God, this is going to be a miracle." She would say to the doctor, "I believe in miracles, don't you?" This patient did fulfill her expectations of a miracle and was able to walk out of the hospital. Later, she sent the staff a picture of herself on horseback. Had this nurse not been able to feel hope for this patient, it would have been very difficult for her to persevere with the rigors of the care required for rehabilitation, and she might not have noticed those subtle signs, such as eye movements or muscle tension that indicate the first signs of responsiveness in a comatose patient.

Being hopeful also requires an appreciation of the human experience and a basic sense of trust in the inherent potential of each client. There is no need to rush in and take over. For a psychiatrist, caring about her clients means "not interfering . . . so they are more free to be themselves," a position that assumes respect for and trust in her clients' own capacity to heal. This orientation allows caregivers to see strengths where others might not.

A social worker, the director of a children's psychiatric unit, described the mother of one of the children he was treating who had a "horrendous background," having been victimized her whole life:

> I couldn't quite figure out how this woman was alive. . . . As a child, she couldn't describe to me one adult male that hadn't sexually

abused her. . . . Yet this mother really did love her son. . . . Even given all that this woman had gone through, she could see clearly that he had a problem and that she had to get help for him. . . . So we directed the treatment around this woman's strengths. . . . Given her horrendous history, her own [history of] alcohol and substance abuse, what was she doing good, what was she doing right.

I really have an appreciation of those kind of people, because I don't understand why people like that haven't . . . committed suicide. . . . You turn that around and realize this was an incredible woman. She had incredible strengths. . . . I can't help but be in awe of her in some capacity. . . . Part of this business about caring is that you have to look at people's strengths.

Lack of Ego Involvement

A distinctive feature of caring communication is the lack of ego involvement on the part of the caregiver. This quality became quite clear during the research process, when informants were describing their experiences. The caregivers talked more about the patients then they did about themselves or what they did.

These expert caregivers allowed themselves to become part of the background rather than the foreground of the patient's experience; therefore, what they did was not always obvious, even to themselves. One nurse describes feeling like the silent conductor, orchestrating all the resources on behalf of the patient. Others explain, "It [caring] puts you more in touch with everyone else, rather than on a pedestal." Another says, "I don't think ego is involved. I think it's at a higher level than the ego because you are not trying to inflate yourself." An oncology nurse describes not wanting to be the center point, or the focal point of the patient's experience: "I'm not the one, they are the one, and . . . if they are strong, they are healthy, they go on and know that they did that—I didn't do it. . . . I appreciate being . . . acknowledged and that . . . but this is their illness experience."

The satisfaction of caring is very different from the sense of achievement we derive from the curing aspect, the technical skills that each discipline offers to clients who seek their services. This curing piece gives caregivers the satisfaction of experiencing their own sense of agency and control by being able to manipulate, fix, or resolve a problem external to self. The heroic aspect to this kind of helping is satisfying to the ego; however, the satisfaction of caring comes from the caregiver's ability to go beyond the limitations of her or his own ego, to experience another person's world, or another way of being that is totally different from the caregiver's.

For example, a psychiatrist, in describing the satisfaction she finds in working with the developmentally disabled, says, "We go into their world for awhile. . . . They enrich my life in that way." A physical therapist describes the tension between caring and curing and how she works to keep the focus on the patient rather than on herself. When she takes a course and learns a new technique that works effectively, it feels good, but

> You have to be careful, because . . . [the focus becomes] me doing things . . . instead of educating the patient and getting the patient involved. . . . This whole dependency thing feeds the ego . . . , so we look at what's happening in their life outside of the clinic, and bring their life on the outside into the clinic. Then they're not so dependent on me.

A psychiatric nurse described how her former ego-centered attempts at caring were driven by a need to excel, increase self-esteem, or prove a point. Now she has learned to draw from what is best in the environment, to "go with the flow . . . pulling more out of an abundance."

Expanded Personal Boundaries

Caring professionals have an expanded sense of self, such that their interests are defined in terms of others, as well as themselves. This expanded self-interest can be understood according to Gilligan's (1982) theory. According to Gilligan, the highest level of moral development in women is characterized by an awareness of our essential interconnectedness and interdependence, such that caring becomes a creative form of self-expression, one that enhances both self and others.

The experience of a psychiatric nurse working in a state hospital illustrates how this predisposition shapes the form of caring. One evening, the nurse was assaulted by a very psychotic patient, who punched her in the face. Despite the fact that she was in pain, with significant facial injuries, and somewhat dazed following the attack, one of her first thoughts was that the other patients would probably be afraid that she would leave and never come back. So before she went home, she called a community meeting and explained to the patients that, although she was injured and upset about the incident, she had no intention of abandoning them and that she would return after she had recovered. Her instinctive response to her own crisis automatically included a concern for those with whom she felt a connection.

During her recovery process, when she was going through the posttrauma response, she had moments when she didn't think that she could ever come back. Part of what helped her to be able to return to work and to heal emotionally from the trauma was, in addition to the caring she received from her co-workers, the concern she had for what her resignation would mean to the other patients on the unit. Now, as she looks back on the incident, she sees it as a positive experience. Her connectedness included her concern for others, as well as being able to receive caring from others.

Note

1. To protect the anonymity of clients, all names have been changed.

Four

Caring in Action

Behavioral Qualities

*C*aring expressed at the behavioral level is characterized by eight properties: (a) empowerment through the mobilization of resources, (b) advocacy, (c) authenticity, (d) responsiveness, (e) commitment, (f) being present with, (g) creating positive meaning and hope, and (h) competence.

Empowerment Through the Mobilization of Resources

Perhaps the most important behavioral manifestation of caring is to empower patients by helping them to mobilize their own resources. Again, the focus is not on what the caregiver does to fix the problem, but instead to facilitate the patients' own inherent capacities for healing. Professional caring means that the caregivers try to work themselves out of the picture.

Caregivers emphasize the importance of having the appropriate resources to meet the patient's needs, and they see their role as orchestrating these resources. The most important resource is the inherent strength and potential of each client. As Chapter 3 showed, caregivers tend to have a hopeful orientation that allows them to see these strengths and the possibilities inherent to the situation.

The focus, then, is to empower the patient by mobilizing these possibilities. Again, expert caregivers do not become the focus for the patient. These caregivers do not see themselves as the most important resource, but rather as the orchestrator of resources. While they may be involved with a patient over a long period of time, the nature of this involvement is transient. As one nurse explains, when working with the families of dying patients, "It's more appropriate for [patients] to get emotional support from their daughters or their sisters or their family members than it is to get it from [a caregiver] who has just been involved in the patient's care when he's dying."

An ICU nurse describes how she tries to help families communicate with each other during the crisis of illness:

> I've made families confront each other. One kid had a severed spinal cord. He and his father hated each other. The kid was in really bad shape. I told them they needed to sit down and talk, and they did. There was some yelling, and then it was okay. Sometimes, when families call . . . they'll say "tell them I called." I'll say, "Is there anything else you'd like to say?" and they'll stammer for a bit, and I'll say, "would you like to tell him you love him," and they start to cry and say "yes."

Another nurse describes how a priest dying of cancer had alienated all of his family, fellow priests, and caregivers. He had a sign posted on his door that said "Do not enter unless you absolutely have something specific to do":

> And so I thought, well this sounds like somebody that probably needs to be seen and I realized I was probably Daniel walking into the lion's den. . . . I went to see him . . . every day after that for two months to the point where I probably became more invested in him than would be considered professional. However, he had no family, his fellow priests were staying away from him, . . . and this man was going through some real issues about his termination because that is how he viewed it, that he was being terminated and he did not want to be alone.

While at first she was his only resource, the only one he would talk to, she quickly extended the support she was giving him to include others. She asked a friend of hers who was an ex-priest to come and talk to him. With the help of this friend, they got his fellow priests reinvolved. They then worked with his physician to contact his sister who was in another state and had no concept of how sick he really was:

> She came and spent two weeks. . . . They had priests with him round the clock, just as friends, to pray with him, to be with him when he woke up in the middle of the night. The man went through such an incredible change over the next couple of weeks and then eventually went into a coma and died on Christmas. But he had had an opportunity to accept and to have closure with his sister and spiritual contact.

By the time of his death, this nurse was no longer the focus; she was able to fade into the background, so those people who were most significant in his life could be there for him.

Advocacy

Because in a health-care situation, clients are always vulnerable, and sometimes helpless, caregivers may have to take a more active role to empower resources on their clients' behalf. A psychologist, whose only job was to do psychotherapy, couldn't ignore the fact that her client had no money for food or medications. She called the business office of the hospital and was able to negotiate a loan and medications for her client until the client's disability check arrived. Similarly, an infectious disease nurse interceded on behalf of an elderly lady when her family wanted her in a nursing home where they knew she'd be "safe." She explains: "I just tried to relate some of the feelings that Mrs. Jones was having [and to give them specific reassurances for each of their concerns.] . . . the reassurances made them feel better. They didn't really trust what she was saying."

Likewise, an oncology nurse describes the kind of advocacy that comes naturally to her when she is, as she describes, "in love" with her patients:

> She believed in me that I would do things for her best interests . . . and she let me see what her best interest was. You know, so she felt safe

to do that. And safety was a real issue for her too. She was one of those people who [would] go home, and in two days . . . be back in the hospital sick with fevers. And [she had] this thing about her skin—taking care of her frail, red hair, translucent, beautiful white skin. [This] was a really big issue for her. And so when she would come on the floor she would look to see who was there and were they going to hurt her. She trusted that I would take care of her skin. . . . And that I would make sure that nobody hurt her skin. . . . And I was able to not have any of the interns and residents start IVs on her, it was either me or [name of doctor], the big chief guy, and that was it.

Sometimes advocacy requires direct conflict and confrontation with others, a position that is uncomfortable for caregivers who tend to value positive relationships. One nurse felt concern for a 12-year-old who started bleeding excessively after having her tonsils removed. The surgeon (whose patients seemed to bleed inappropriately a lot) took a long needle and injected the back of her throat while she was still awake. The nurse said:

Surely you are going to take her back and put her to sleep to do that, but he said "no, no." I was very upset and I did say something to the parents about the fact that she could have nightmares from that. . . . I mean I had nightmares so I'm sure she did too . . . and [the parents] asked me . . . whether or not I would go to [that doctor]. . . . And I tried to answer the questions I could without being direct, but I did not feel that I could be dishonest with the family. So . . . they did change doctors. I was glad because I really thought that this was safest for this child . . . , but I almost got sued by the doctor.

The doctor served her with a formal intent to sue but later withdrew his intent. Her relationship with him, however, continues to be quite stressful. "I'm not real good when confronted with a negative situation. . . . I like win/win situations." Yet the fact that she cared brought out the courage to take on a conflict she would have preferred to avoid.

Authenticity

Chapter 3 showed how expert caregivers are willing to cross the line demarcating professional role boundaries. This section of this chapter shows the form that this personal honesty assumes in the behavioral dimension. Reaching out from behind the professional persona, expert caregivers make an effort to become involved in a more personal way. This sometimes takes the form of humor and displays of affection. For example, a psychologist threw wadded-up pieces of tissue at her adolescent client when she became angry with him during a therapy session.

Nevertheless, if caregivers are frustrated because they feel angry or alienated by a patient's behavior, they must address these feelings in a way that still will allow them to be able to feel genuine concern and to stay in relationship with the patient. This may involve some type of confrontation. The difference between a caring and a noncaring confrontation is that a caring confrontation is motivated by the sincere desire to stay in relationship, to stay involved in a way that is helpful to the patient. This confrontation is an alternative to detachment or emotional withdrawal.

For example, a medical-surgical nurse felt that one of the differences between caring and just taking care of someone's physical needs is being involved enough to be able to share how she feels about the patient. She needs to be able to share negative as well as positive feelings: "To be able to say, 'it makes me really upset and angry when you say that.'" A psychiatric nurse pointed out the importance of

> going on something that is genuine instead of something that is drummed up in the name of caring—that I'm supposed to care about somebody I really don't care about— . . . I think is much more harmful to the patient than not caring about them if that's a genuine response.

This nurse also described how she deals with not liking a patient:

> I guess I have learned to relax about it. And usually if that's ok with me then I usually do start liking the patient at some point along the line, especially if I can, in a not annihilating sort of way, honestly say to the patient, "you know when you do this particular thing I kind of experience that as distancing." That . . . by being honest about that, and . . . I mean it's not total gut reaction feedback . . . it's not me saying . . . I can't stand you, but . . . there is a distance between us and . . . this is my reaction.

This same nurse then pointed out the dangers of going overboard with authenticity. She always had difficulty working with developmentally disabled individuals. The caring did not come naturally to her when working with these clients. One day, as she said, she "lost it" and started screaming at a patient who had smeared the room with feces, accusing her of acting like an animal. "I feel like I just absolutely in the rawest sense of the word went with my gut, and I guess I don't think there is anything bad with having those feelings, it was more what I did with it." In this case, her confrontation of the patient was not motivated by a desire to stay in relationship in a way that was helpful to the patient. Instead, it was just a raw expression of her own negative feelings and reactions. Now, as a result of that experience, she is more cautious of her gut response, especially with those clients she feels conflicted about: "I guess I see good interactions as being a balance of both things, of being able to use your head and use your gut at the same time."

A rehabilitation nurse describes an even more controversial situation, but one which she perceived as caring. A patient who was quadriplegic had ordered an aide not to lower the head of his bed as she was preparing him for sleep. The aide refused because she knew that it would put pressure on his coccyx, which would lead to skin breakdown. He called her a "fucking bitch." The rehabilitation nurse wouldn't stand for that lack of respect for her staff, so she went in and told him that she wouldn't tolerate that. She said that if he wouldn't let the aide lower his head, she would, and she proceeded to lower the bed. He began yelling and threatened to have her name in the local newspaper, and she said, "fine, but tonight you're going to be quiet and let everyone else in this room sleep." He replied, "well I'm going to hit this bell constantly all night." She then responded, "well, I'll just put the bell where you can't reach it then," and she did.

He then asserted his power by reporting her to the administration, and she was reprimanded by the director of nursing. She apologized for letting other patients and her staff witness the interaction but felt confident that she had done the right thing. The patient and she became good friends, and she would often turn the pages of a book for him while he read before falling asleep. I asked her if she would have been able to become friends with this patient had she felt inhibited in being able to respond to him. She replied, "well, probably not. I'd be angry at myself and him. You have to be firm and do what's best."

Now, of course, we don't have the patient's perception of this incident to confirm whether he saw it in the same way; however, based on the perceived outcome, it might be conjectured that this tussle was *ego syntonic* (meaning that it was consistent with both of their personalities and the way that they handled conflict) and that it provided the catharsis necessary for both of them to remain involved with each other during the intensity required of a rehabilitation experience. While taking a patient's call light is not recommended as a caring practice, it is possible that a good, honest spat between a caregiver and patient, providing neither one holds a disproportionate amount of power, is preferable to the potential feelings of alienation created by being surrounded by dispassionate professionals.

Responsiveness

Responsiveness means that caregivers are very attuned to and accommodate to the subtleties that present themselves in the moment with a particular patient, rather than acting on their own preconceived ideas of what would be helpful. Chapter 1 showed how caregivers have a sensitivity to the human vulnerability inherent in health care. A speech pathologist showed how that sensitivity manifests itself, when she rocked and sang to a child who was upset when she tried to do speech drills with him. As a result of her responsiveness, the child began to sing with her, which was the first time she had heard him make an intentional sound.

This level of responsiveness involves sensitivity to subtle nonverbal cues. For example, the operating room nurse explains how she meets her patients before surgery and extends what appears to be a professional handshake, but by noticing whether they pull back, she senses at what level they need to be emotionally connected to her; and by reading faces, she tries to get a sense whether there is unfinished business with families that may require a little more time before surgery.

A recovery room nurse let 56 relatives onto the ICU to be with an elderly Hispanic man who was dying. She responded not only to the need of this large extended family to be with this man as he lay dying, but also to the technology in a very human way. The patient was on a heart monitor, so she could see his cardiac activity and noticed that his heart beat fluctuated in response to the family's grieving:

> Every time the whole family prayed for him and everybody would kneel down for the rosary . . . and his heart beat would get faster . . . and then they would start talking to each other and . . . his blood pressure would go back down, his heart, his QRSs would widen out, so I talked to one of the family members and told him that I think he is trying to come back into this world. . . . [to] say, "it's okay to let me go," but he loves you . . . so I explained my feelings about the death process to him and . . . it was okay for him to go.

The family later showed up with a 40-pound fruit basket to express their gratitude, explaining that their last visit with him gave them such a "good sense of peace and such a sense of joy."

Responsiveness to the subtler human elements of a situation includes efforts to maintain the dignity of patients by giving extra attention to grooming, comfort, and privacy needs. An ICU nurse explains:

> I like to see patients, especially the horribly sick patients, feel good about themselves. You know, keep people straightened up and looking like somebody is taking care of them. I have a real hard time working with nurses, where their patients are trashed out. You know the patient has no self . . . , just make them look nice, like somebody cares about them.

A medical-surgical nurse says,

> I always talk to them, whether they are . . . in a coma, if they are completely confused, for whatever reason I still talk to them, you know, who knows. I'm not to say what is going on in there, so I just talk to them . . . like what the weather is outside, what I'm going to do, I talked to your sons today, you know, things like that. . . . And keeping them covered up . . . respecting their modesty . . . whatever their mental state . . . adds to their dignity.

This responsive mode of communication allows for a more accommodating response to patients labeled as difficult or demanding.

Requests tend to be taken at face value without a lot of value judgments and interpretations. A fairly recent graduate said, "Some nurses describe patients in blunt terms, like trouble-maker, but I don't have that same perception. I don't know why." She described one patient whose family expected special privileges because the daughter had a fairly high position at the hospital. The daughter was threatening to the staff because she was vigilant and critical of the care being given. This nurse responded to the daughter's request for a bibliography on her mother's illness "to see if they were missing anything." The patient died 2 days after she compiled the bibliography and gave it to the daughter. The nurse was glad that she had respected her request as a valid one.

Responsiveness also involves anticipating the patient's needs. "I can almost know what a patient will ask me and I will do it before they ask me." This nurse was distressed by the nonresponsive behavior she sees in many new graduates: "They are not seeing, they are not seeing the things that patients need and the care that they need. It's like they are oblivious to it."

This responsiveness also involves humanizing the experience for patients. A psychiatric social worker tries to imagine how parents must feel when they have to admit their child to a psychiatric facility. He tries to establish a collegial relationship with them so that they don't feel scrutinized and intimidated. An ICU nurse describes how he tries to humanize the experience of the ICU:

> I tend to not try to act like an ultraprofessional, which just . . . alienates them, makes them feel much more like a patient . . . and just makes them feel really sick. . . . [I also] try to get patients' families away from being mesmerized by the monitor . . . kind of relax the environment a little bit. . . . There [are] beepers and buzzers and everything else; you just have to get patients and families relaxed and have them not orient on that.

An operating room nurse describes specific behaviors intended to calm patients in the surgical environment:

> And when I get them alone, once I have them settled on the operating bed and I've done all the professional things that I need to do and as they are going off to sleep, then I take their hand again. Sometimes I even lay my other hand on their faces, sometimes, it depends on the age of the patient and the comfort level of the patient, and what I'm

feeling from them. And then I usually make eye contact before they go off to sleep and say at the same time, "you know we are going to be taking very good care of you, you are healthy, and we are going to see you when you wake up in recovery," because I like to reinforce the idea in their minds that I expect them to wake up. A lot of people come in with an unspoken fear of dying from anesthesia.

Commitment

Commitment is evidenced by going "beyond the call of duty." As one nurse says, "When an individual cares, they go out of their way, especially when the patient is so alone." A burn nurse explains, "I think you put forth that extra maybe 110% effort instead of just 100% if you are getting involved and you care." For example, she will call "someone at night to see if they are still okay after they have been in for a day surgery procedure, or stop by and pick up a bottle of baby shampoo as opposed to using what the hospital had." This nurse sometimes gave families her home phone number so they could call her if they had trouble with the burn dressings. On one occasion, she had a mother bring the child to her home so that she could check the dressing.

Commitment involves doing those little extras. An ICU nurse came in on his day off with rollers and a blow dryer to style the hair of a cancer patient who had told him that it would make her feel so much better if she could get her hair styled before her surgery. Another ICU nurse sang songs and gave foot soaks to her patients who were comatose. She joked that she thought they got better faster, so they could wake up and tell her to stop singing. After her shift is over, an operating room nurse briefly stops by the rooms of those patients who had had surgery just to say "Hi," and to see how they are doing. A psychologist, on her own time, spent an afternoon to be with her client and offer support as she went with detectives to revisit the scene of a crime where she had been brutally victimized.

Being Present With the Patient

Just being present with a patient is a powerful way to communicate caring. One caregiver observes that "when I come across someone, and there is a wall, I [think] that what the person needs is not so much verbally what you say to them, but the presence of someone caring." Many health professionals are taught that their tasks or technical skills are the only way of helping that has value. An occupational therapist comments, "It took me a long time to figure out that it was just okay to be there." For one nurse being with a patient was expressed by taking her paperwork into the patient's room and finishing it at the bedside instead of at the nursing station. A psychiatrist recalls working with a developmentally disabled woman who "didn't say more than three words to me for about eight months. . . . She was absolutely silent. . . . So just sitting on the sofa with this woman and her saying nothing, and just waiting. . . . It was a long wait. . . . Now she talks a blue streak."

The presence of someone is important as people make the transition from life to death. An ICU nurse said, "I'm a firm believer in not letting people die alone, so I'll be there with them, and I'll hold their hand." A medical-surgical nurse manager described her interaction with a dying patient's daughter:

> And I just stayed with her and she said "do something, do something!" and I said "What do you want me to do? Do you really want me to do something to save his life?" And she kind of looked at me, and I said "You know we can't do that, there is nothing we can do for him" and she said "Yes," and I said, "but I can be here with you." So she just put her arm around me, and I put my arm around her, and we just stood there, and she held his hand, and it was over in maybe five minutes. . . . And she came to me afterwards . . . and she said "The fact that you stayed there helped me."

Creating Positive Meaning and Hope

As Chapter 3 showed, caregivers tend to have a hopeful disposition that lends itself to finding meaning and possibilities in tragic circumstances. This meaning is necessary for the caregiver not only to be able to tolerate being involved in these situations, but also to sustain hope for the patient and family. This section shows how these caregivers work with their patients to create the kinds of meanings that lend themselves to hopefulness and healing.

For an occupational therapist, creating meaning during a child's rehabilitation experience is an integral part of the healing for that child. She has helped to develop programs, such as a summer camp that is

> geared toward establishing meaning for the child—and then the healing will come. We have a camp . . . where we take the kids up and do rock climbing and canoeing and we sleep out in tepees, and we try and build this culture that has a lot of meaningful things in it and then, despite themselves, the kids are . . . integrating on a sensory level because the things are meaningful for them.

Meaning, then, is what organizes the experience for the child and what mobilizes the healing process.

Meaning is also used in a more existential way, to provide significance to a person's life. For a young man dying of AIDS, who had been rejected and abandoned by his family, his nurse said, "It's important that his caregivers really think he's a wonderful human being." Another described how she tries to make a "person's life more valuable when you know they don't have very much time left . . . you are able to show that he was an important person and that you really care."

As Chapter 3 showed, a rehabilitation nurse had a hopeful orientation that sustained her during her work with a young woman who was described as a "vegetable" following a brain stem stroke. Here is how she created the meaning that allowed her to feel hope and optimism while working with this client:

> When she first came I thought "oh my goodness!" You know when we saw what she couldn't do. The only thing she could do was really follow you with her eyes and the tears. . . . But I felt just, well, when [the doctor] came, he said, "what do you think," and I said, "well I think if she came here at least she has a chance. I think if you leave her she's got nothing."

As you may recall, this patient did recover and later sent a picture of herself riding a horse.

Some situations create even more of a challenge to find positive meaning. A psychiatric nurse works with people with dissociative disorders (multiple personality disorder or MPD), believed to be caused by a history of severe child abuse. In some cases, the patients were brought up in satanic cults where ritualistic torture and human sacrifice were practiced. Instead of becoming lost in the horror of the abuse, she tries to stay focused on the human element, where she can always find some basis for hope.

One client who was very withdrawn and fearful of being touched by anyone revealed, during a session with this nurse, a very painful childhood memory of being forced to participate in the mutilation and subsequent death of a childhood friend. At the end of the conversation, which was quite difficult for both of them, the nurse made a connection between this experience and her fear of getting close to people: "I mean this girl can't even touch somebody's hand, so I encouraged her to try and touch . . . my hand . . . after having to work through her memory so horrendous as that, . . . and she had a very difficult time but she kind of lightly touched." The interaction ended, in spite of its content, on a positive hopeful note.

This same nurse gives another example of creating new meaning and hope with a client who had a great deal of difficulty accepting her mother's death. This client frequently became suicidal and talked about wanting to go to heaven to be with her mother. The nurse was helping this client plan a memorial service in which "she's going to send off a balloon and at the bottom of the balloon she's going to tie a message that's going to go to heaven for her mom."

Competence

Skilled competence is an integral part of the communication of caring in health care. Because of their vulnerability, patients need to be assured of their caregivers' competence before they can trust. One nurse describes the development of her relationship with a patient: "And then came the trust that develops between a patient and a nurse. 'I know that you can take care of me because you know what you are doing and because what you have done in the past has worked out well.'"

Some health-care professionals in highly technical areas assume that emotional detachment is necessary in order to be able to function competently. In acute medical situations, technical skills are primary, and the relational aspects of caring are sometimes viewed as getting in the way of the technical skill and objectivity required. An ICU nurse describes his experience with novice practitioners who get too emotionally involved:

> You see someone arrest and they have been taken care of by someone, by a nurse or whatever who got too involved in the case and the person arrests and they just freeze. I think that as you get better at being a practitioner of the physical, taking care of the physical aspects of the patients, you can pay more attention to the psycho-social needs. . . . But that comes with experience and you still have to keep the physical elements as the primary focus.

While this concern is important, it suggests that the problem is the lack of technical expertise rather than the involvement per se. The experiences of expert caregivers challenge the idea that emotional detachment is necessary for technical competence, at least within the context of a professional caring relationship. An operating room nurse, a practitioner who perhaps represents the most technical context, explains: "My technical skills aren't down because of what I do [getting involved] because actually the goal of my technical skills is also to maintain that integrity [of the person]." An occupational therapist explains that caring "seemed to draw from me skills and ways of being." She learns technical skills better when she cares, because when she has a feeling of engagement with her clients, "I usually integrate it [the skill] into my whole being."

The oncology nurse who described the advocacy that comes naturally to her when she is "in love" with her patients believes that her feelings of love and protectiveness were what allowed her to perform venipuncture with exquisite accuracy, so that she would minimize trauma to her patient with the very delicate skin. "I don't think I'm any better necessarily than anybody else, but for some reason . . . [when I feel] professional nursing love [I can] perform technical kinds of intrusive things with skill and with great aplomb." Another nurse who was a recent graduate also felt that caring enhanced her technical performance: "It's like I have a bee in my bonnet. . . . I'm sharper, more with it. . . . I have to get involved for the rest of it to make sense."

These findings are consistent with Benner's (1984) study of skill development in nursing, mentioned in Chapter 1. As you may recall, Benner found that the engagement and attentiveness characteristic of caring are essential for the intuitive level of understanding that characterizes expert practitioners in highly technical fields. In fact, the caring seems to be the gestalt, the overriding framework that draws out and organizes the skills and knowledge needed to be effective with a given client. The speech therapist who rocked and sang to the child who was screaming allowed her feelings of caring for this child to lead her response. Later, she discovered a theory—sensory integration—that would explain why her intervention was helpful. She continues to discover creative new methods of helping people, but she is led to these methods through her relationships with the clients. She says "that's the only way I know."

An occupational therapist uses a biological metaphor of cell division to explain how caring draws the knowledge from her:

> When the cells line up along the spindles, . . . there is something that magnetizes them to divide. What it felt like was that things . . . were being magnetized out of me. A sense of caring. A sense of humor. A sense of just kind of knowing how to work with his [patient's] frustration, or his difficulties in a way that honored where he was at but also helped him to get to a different place. And all that stuff was magnetized out of me without me putting in a lot of conscious effort. . . . It felt easy. . . . There is that tangible feeling of caring, all of a sudden you are thinking more globally, and you're thinking more elegantly in some way, and therefore the decisions are made because to not respect the process . . . feels annoying. It feels incomplete.

Five

Caring Unfolds With the Client

Relational Qualities

Caring involves more than its behavioral manifestations. Some qualities of caring are not necessarily visible and can only be understood from a relational perspective. These qualities will unfold in a unique way as each relationship develops; therefore, they cannot be predicted or prescribed ahead of time. Implicit throughout this chapter is that the form of this relationship will be determined by the uniqueness of each person involved. The participation of the patient, implied throughout this chapter, is as important as the participation of the caregiver; however, the focus here is on the role of the caregiver. Additional information related to the patient's participation is presented in Chapter 10. The relational qualities of caring include (a) deep emotional involvement, (b) self-awareness and purposeful use of self, (c) intersubjectivity, (d) aesthetic qualities, and (e) transcendent qualities.

Deep Emotional Involvement

Caring is seen by caregivers as a "deeper expression and deeper relationship of yourself with somebody else . . . and it's okay to be emotional about it." In fact, many of the clinicians became teary or cried openly when telling their stories. A counselor's experience has been that "these people have broken my heart, softened my heart, and broken through a lot of my pride."

The term *love* is frequently used. A rehabilitation nurse described caring as "unconditional love. . . . I think it's hard to stay distant from patients. If you feel for them, you are going to enter into their experience whether you want to or not. It's just something that you do." An occupational therapist explains, "They used to tell us, if you got too involved with a person it isn't good therapy. I think the reverse is true. If you're not involved enough, it's not good therapy."

The words *bond, intimacy,* and *connection* are also used. This intense closeness may develop over time during the course of the relationship but often occurs during brief contacts within an intense context of life and death (this distinctive quality of the health-care environment is discussed further in the next chapter).

The psychologist who spent a day with her client and the detectives to visit the scene of a crime in which her client had been brutally victimized was willing to do this because "sometimes you have to match the courage of your patients." She believes in the value of being authentic with her clients, especially those who may have never experienced a healthy relationship.

A counselor on a psychiatric unit who had training as a lay minister became deeply involved with a woman diagnosed with MPD, and he played a significant role in helping her make peace with her inner turmoil:

> I would spend a lot of time with her. She would request [individual sessions] with me. They were very heavy. I felt real close, but it felt like an okay thing. I felt genuinely interested and hopeful for her. [but] there were times when I was home and I'd start crying thinking about her torment. I really wanted her to be free of this torment.

Traditional wisdom would caution caregivers against becoming so involved, especially with someone suffering from such a complex disorder. However, this clinician was able to handle this intensity in a way that worked for himself and for his client, despite his fears of overinvolvement. Chapter 7 returns to an exploration of this situation and examines more closely the skills necessary for working within such a deep level of involvement.

Self-Awareness and Purposeful Use of Self

The deep level of involvement just described requires a very sophisticated level of self-understanding. The caregiver must process the subjective elements of the relationship, including his or her own personal experiences and feelings, so that they are expressed in a caring rather than an ego-centered way. For example, the counselor who worked with the client with MPD realizes his own vulnerability to the many ways in which he could be seduced away from staying in a therapeutic role with his clients. A nurse realizes her tendency to take over and do too much for patients, but, as she says, "I'm learning. I'm always learning. Never stop learning."

As the next chapter shows, it is very difficult to do this type of self-examination in isolation from others. Caregivers need to talk to others and to see themselves in the context of a team. A rehabilitation nurse has observed that an indication that persons on the team have become overinvolved is that these persons stop talking to others and stop ventilating their own feelings.

This ongoing self-examination and sorting out of emotional reactions is illustrated by the psychiatric nurse who, during a goal-setting group, had such a strong emotional response to the apathy of a suicidal patient (see Chapter 3). As you may recall, she "felt like putting my head on my hands and bawling my eyes out." Her first reaction to her emotional response was

> I found myself holding my breath and going "Holy Toledo!" this is a really strange reaction. So I decided to find out whether or not it was in fact some kind of countertransference on my part, so I kind of opened up my body and started scanning the group to see if this had affected other people.

She explained that opening up her body and scanning the group was an instinctive way to get outside of herself and her own reactions. When she did this, she saw one patient who was so suicidal she had tied a shoelace around her neck so tightly that it had broken the blood vessels in her face, another patient whose eating disorder behavior was totally out of control, and another patient who had been forced to give up 30 years of amphetamine abuse and was left with nothing:

And so all of a sudden it really hit me that this was the theme for the group, it wasn't just my experience with Bob. And so I decided to go ahead and go with what I was feeling, and . . . I didn't do what I instinctively wanted to do which was sob, but I looked and I said to the group, "You know I'm just having a real strong reaction to something that is going on in the group and I feel like I need to deal with it, and so I turned and I looked at Bob, and tears came to my eyes and I said, "You know, Bob, I feel like I'm losing you and I don't know what to do."

Rather than detaching herself from her intense emotional response, this nurse examined her feelings in terms of a larger context beyond herself. This larger context or broader perspective that caregivers have access to comes from the knowledge base of their discipline, the caregiver's own life experience, lessons learned from other patients, and the shared perspective of the team or other colleagues.

Intersubjectivity

The depth of involvement in a caring relationship requires that both the caregiver and client are active participants in creating the relationship, and both are affected by the experience. When clinicians who were interviewed talked about caring, they always talked about how they were affected by the experience. A social worker describes how lucky he feels for having the opportunity to work with troubled children and their families. "I have learned a tremendous amount from these people . . . and you can't help but change yourself. . . . I have always felt like if I don't go into therapy with someone, and come out a different person, it's a signal that I probably need to really take stock and move out of the arena of mental health."

Caregivers are often inspired by patients. The social worker feels admiration and "awe" for his clients who have survived so much abuse. A psychologist also is amazed that some of her clients are still alive: "They take my breath away." This appreciation for the patient is sometimes communicated directly. For example, one nurse says, "I was able to share how I felt about how they were affecting me. Like Pat, to be able to tell her, 'I really have enjoyed taking care of you. I enjoy you as a person. You have meant a lot to me.'" Another explains: "This is my life too and they are impacting on my life. I don't want them to not know that they are part of how I live and how I feel even though in this instance their needs are why we are there."

Reciprocity on the part of the patient, including expressions of gratitude and appreciation, are a part of the intersubjective experience. Often, the rewards are obvious and take the form of words, cards, or gifts; however, sometimes the appreciation is less obvious. A hospice nurse's most significant caring experience involved a rather odd 40-year-old single woman who lived "a rather non-verbal life" with her brother. They were both very unattractive, particularly the brother, who had great big lumps on his face, and their apartment was filthy. The sister had a malignant tumor in her thigh, but she refused amputation, so the tumor grew. Her leg eventually became bigger than her body trunk, and about a month before she died, it ruptured, leaving a big hole and a lot of very smelly drainage. This woman "hardly ever talked. There was never any eye contact." In spite of the unappealing nature of the situation, the caregivers became very attached to this woman and learned "a deeper appreciation of people who can't express themselves, because in her own way . . . I think she loved us all because of what we gave to her."

> She could never say things like . . . "thank you" for anything. I mean I'd bring her a sandwich and sit down and eat and that was it. She never said thank you. But it wasn't necessary and I never felt put upon because she didn't say thank you. That's just the kind of person she was. And I get very insulted with some people when they don't say that but it didn't matter with her because she . . . gave us . . . a lot in her nonverbal communication with us.

About 6 weeks before she died, the nurse, the volunteer, and the home health aide brought dinner and a cake and streamers over for her birthday. It was the first time she ever talked. She talked about her childhood and told some very funny stories, which was totally out of character for her. "She came alive, and she appreciated [what we had done]. She could never say it because she didn't know how. Nobody had ever given her anything before. It showed her that people cared and really, all of us dearly loved her."

The paradoxical element of reciprocity is that it is not expected, and while appreciation is important to morale, it is not seen as an essential part of the relationship. An occupational therapist explains, "The involvement is to love and to care without expecting anything back, and to feel yourself as kind of a conduit." A medical-surgical head nurse observed that some new graduates expect too much in terms of reciprocity:

> If you expect to get a lot back from [a] patient, you won't always get it because that's the nature of [it]—when people are sick they don't say thank you. . . . You have to find something in it that makes you feel good. . . . There is a certain something in you that enjoys communicating with another human being, yet is not discouraged if that other human being doesn't return something. . . . It's a mind set, an inner thing that you feel good about.

A rehabilitation nurse feels that caring has to be done for its own sake, "It seems like the right thing to do. That is your satisfaction. It's its own reason for doing things."

Aesthetic Qualities

Caring has an inherent aesthetic quality that feels effortless and correct, as though the communication is in keeping with a larger sense of order. A nurse says, "I pull together a beautiful symphony." An occupational therapist describes her involvement with a group of children at summer camp: "It felt good. It felt easy. I was a part of something that was beautiful." Another explains, "It is a dance, between me and the child. . . . True therapy is an art, a blend of science and art. . . . Otherwise you might as well be working on an assembly line at General Motors."

When the relationship is right, there is a flow, harmony, and easiness to the caregiver's involvement. A physical therapist describes it as getting on the same rhythm with another person. To be sensitive to another person's rhythms begins by establishing a connection, using one's senses. This may start with the eyes. "I would just look at the individual in their eyes, just really watch how they looked at me, and how they talked to me." She describes her attempts to work with a 4-year-old child who was quadriplegic and dependent on a ventilator to breath. She could tell by his eyes that "his fears were overwhelming." Earlier in her career, she would have been focused on what she needed to do, and "if he screams or yells, that's normal." Now, however, as she has become expert in the art of her work she works to establish synchrony with her actions and his response:

> Just sitting there and touching parts of him where I know his sensation was intact, doing the examination of him, [I] just started very lightly touching in those areas until I could get some trust, and it was clear that when he looked at me, when I told him what I was going to do, that it was okay. . . . I could judge what was okay and what wasn't okay.

This description is very similar to Gendron's analysis, from Chapter 2, in which she uses the metaphor of orchestral music to describe the aesthetic form of caring. This example clearly shows the harmonious and synchronous interaction that Gendron describes. To further apply Gendron's framework, it is evident that the therapist's polarity is positive, the temperature is warmth, the force is gentle, the texture-shape is smooth and soft, and the directionality is toward the other, open and giving.

The knowledge and competence that is created by the relationship is also tied to aesthetics. Intuition arises from this harmony and flow with the patient. When all of this is in place, there is a sense that everything is right; the caregiver knows how to respond without having to consciously analyze or process the information. As one psychologist explains, even with her most difficult clients, when this aesthetic connection is in place, the therapy is "just kind of sailing along . . . and I don't have to think a lot during the process. I'm just kind of there."

An occupational therapist compares her work with children to improvisational music:

> If the right players are working together and there is the right feeling, it's obvious where you are supposed to go even though you are creating something that has never been created before, because out of that situation the forms emerge. . . . It's obvious [where you are to go]. It's based on this intuitive sense of proportion and placement and timing and texture. And . . . it's very relational to what the other people are doing. . . . I'm working with a kid, and it becomes this

improvisational dance where the treatment objectives are the things that we are both going towards, and the kid and I are playing in such a way that we are moving towards those . . . and you are drawing upon all of your resources. . . . It becomes very artful.

Transcendent Qualities

As these chapters have shown, caring is characterized by a lack of ego involvement on the part of the caregiver. Instead of experiencing themselves as isolated individuals doing something to or for another person, caregivers, by entering into the world of another, allow themselves to become part of something greater than themselves. As one caregiver says, "I could be larger than my little self." Another says,

> You lose yourself, and also you find it. You feel yourself as you really are, but you kind of lose track of what your face looks like, or whether you combed your hair, and what kind of clothes you put on that day. I guess you're more aware of how you fit into the whole. . . . And there's an awful lot of joy in that.

The nurse who previously had talked about her ability to be nonjudgmental describes how, by entering into a caring relationship, she has the opportunity to "experience a thousand different lifetimes through someone else's eyes." So, the relationship is larger than the individuals involved, it is representative of a larger reality or a larger truth.

For some, this larger truth is experienced at a very spiritual level. As one nurse observes,

> Spiritualness is important. I don't define that according to any particular religion, it comes from a deep sense of ministration to the individual. You minister to the spirit within the body. Sometimes you will not even recognize the person outwardly because of the deterioration. You minister to the spirit. . . . I wasn't aware of that 20 years ago, and I think for many nurses it's dormant. Nursing has helped me to discover that.

Similarly, the psychiatrist who works with severely retarded adults explains the joy she finds in her work; by looking beyond the appearance, she can see that "there's a spirit in every one of these people."

A medical surgical nurse describes how being a Christian gives meaning to the work that she does: "It's where God wants me and . . . by asking God everyday to renew that commitment, it's like a commitment of Him, it makes me look at people differently." For another nurse, doing missionary work on the Gaza Strip challenged her fundamentalist religious beliefs, and she was forced to create her own meaning. Now she describes feeling "more connected to humanity in general." Another nurse was affected by her experience with a "very Catholic nurse" when they were working with refugees in Thailand: She came away from that experience feeling that "people who are in these situations are in a state of grace or in a state of holiness. And so I do think it is a privilege . . . and an honor to be able to be with people like that."

A psychiatric nurse explains how her earlier attempts at caring were characterized by trying to excel, to gain self-esteem, to prove a point, or to "jack yourself up"—in other words, trying to "have that experience for myself." Now that she has matured, she describes her caring as drawing from what is best in the environment, "going with the flow and being there," or "pulling more out of abundance."

This idea of pulling from abundance implies that caregivers draw on a greater source, one that sustains them and serves as a source of energy and self-renewal. The energy needed for caring is perceived to come from a greater source beyond the self. One nurse says, "I don't know how to sustain it without that connection with something greater." Another says: "There is an endless amount of love of God for people, so I don't even worry about that. . . . I really feel like there is a wealth of love that God has given to the whole, to everybody and it's available to be used. And so I can love these people with my whole heart." Another says, "I feel tremendous love for a patient and I feel that they genuinely love me and it seems like it comes from some sort of higher place, that's it's driven from . . . a nurturing place that I think is kind of beyond myself" (Montgomery, 1991a, 1991b, 1992).

Caring Is Contextual

The Health-Care Environment

*A*s we have seen, caring is not an individual accomplishment in which the helper succeeds by achieving mastery over a client's problem. This independent approach to helping represents curing rather than caring. While curing may take away or solve a problem for someone, caring is a participatory act, in which the focus is on empowering the client's own resources for healing or for solving the problem. Caring, then, is expressed through meaningful *participation* in an experience with a client, rather than trying to control the outcome. This means that the nature of the experience itself and the participation of others is as important in shaping the communication as the behavior of the individual caregiver. So, while both caring and curing functions are part of the health-care professional's role, the caring function is more dependent on context.

Although the study on which this text is based did not seek to uncover all of the contextual factors that affect the communication of caring, certain qualities became apparent from the caregivers' accounts, and they deserve to be mentioned, as they illustrate how caring cannot be separated from its context. Further research is needed to explicate the effects of context; however, for now, three significant features of the context must be considered as an integral part of the experience of caring. First is the intensity of the circumstances inherent to the health-care environment itself. Second, most of the care that is provided in these settings is done in the context of a team, so participation at this level also must be considered. Finally, the patients' participation must be acknowledged, for their participation will also determine what form caring will take and whether a caring relationship is even possible.

The Intense Nature of the Health-Care Context

The caring incidents that have been presented thus far have been characterized by crisis, trauma, suffering, loss, and death. These situational factors are compounded by the extreme vulnerability of the patient under these conditions. While these qualities are most apparent in acute and emergent care settings, they are to some degree present in any situation in which clients feel vulnerable. These qualities of the health-care context affect the communication process by allowing almost instantaneous bonding and heightening the power of the communication. Some of the most powerful situations presented here have occurred in settings such as the operating or recovery room, where trust between caregiver and patient does not have the opportunity to develop over time, but seems to be replaced by a need to be instantaneously connected, due to the patient's vulnerability.

An emergency room nurse explained:

> Nurses always have intimate and intense contact, and it's incredibly transient, especially in the emergency room, where you spend only one or two hours with someone, but it's never superficial. You develop an emotional attachment. They have to do that with you. It's part of their survival. You have to allow that. Even if it's negative. [Even] if they push you away they do respond to you in some way. But they usually glom onto you for their survival until they get a hold on what's happening.

Here we can see that in a crisis, trust seems to be an immediate survival instinct rather than something that develops over time during the course of a therapeutic relationship. So rather than having to work to develop trust over time, the clinician in these circumstances needs to appreciate and not interfere with the attachment that is already there.

An operating room (OR) nurse illustrates the instantaneous connection that can occur under these circumstances:

> We had a man who was in his late 60s . . . who came to the OR . . . knowing he was going to have cardiac bypass surgery. And as he was lying on the table, I make it a practice—and I'm not alone in that—to take hold of the patient's hand as they are going to sleep and just to ask them if they have a vacation that they can remember that they would like to take again or some place they would like to be that they can hold in their mind as they are going off to sleep. And what he said to me as he took my hand was, "Actually, what I really could use right now is a hug," and so we, the anesthesiologist just stopped doing anything and I said, "Absolutely, that's one of the free things that you get as a part of your hospitalization here" and bent over and hugged him, and that was a prolonged thing. That was not just a real quickie touch-me, get-off-of-me type of thing. And clearly it was exactly what he needed because after that there was no longer any tension in his face [or] even nervous twitter he had been doing since the moment he came into the room.

The intense nature of the circumstances gave a simple hug from a stranger quite a bit of power.

Another example also illustrates how the intense circumstances enhance the power of the communication. A 4-year-old boy named Jason had been admitted to the hospital with Burkitt's lymphoma, a particularly fast-growing cancer, and was not doing well. He had become mute and withdrawn and was not responding to treatment. In fact, he had not spoken to anyone since he had been in the hospital. The doctors and the staff were afraid they were going to lose him:

> One evening—he wasn't my patient, but I went by his room and saw him laying there, and I don't know how I knew this, but something said to me that he needed to be held right then. I asked him if he would like to rock in the rocking chair, and of course he didn't answer but he did not resist when I picked him up. We sat in that rocking chair for an hour and a half, and I could feel him settling in. I had on this knit sweater with a print, and when he finally sat up I laughed and said "Jason, you've got waffles on your face!" He said "I know, I've

got them on my knees too." That was the first time he spoke, and after that we couldn't shut him up.

This incident proved to be a turning point for this child, and not only did he talk, but he also showed more energy and started responding to treatments. The significance of this incident is that it shows again how the context gives a simple nonverbal communication quite a bit of power. Rocking a child who is distressed is not that unusual and had probably been done before. What may have made the difference is the timing of the response, and the availability of the nurse, both situationally and emotionally. Situationally, she was there in the evening after most other professional staff had left. Evenings are the time when people, especially children, are most likely to seek comfort. A professional who sees patients in an office would not have had access to this intimacy. Emotionally, the nurse also was affected by this intimate context; living with the patient for 8 or 12 hours a day allowed her to see that something was different. She was simply moved by something about him and responded from her heart as well as her intellect.

Team Participation

The participation of others is an intrinsic part of caring. Although several instances were presented in which caring occurred outside the context of a supportive team, caring is more likely to occur within teams that foster a matrix or a web of supportive connections among team members. First, this section looks at the support that is necessary to sustain the caregiver's involvement, and then it explores the support that is necessary to carry out the caring.

Caregiver-Centered Support

As this text has shown, caring is not an individual achievement but a communication that arises spontaneously from its unique context. It is most likely to emerge from within a web of caring, a context that is characterized by connection and concern. An occupational therapist reflects on her experiences with teams that inspired caring. When she worked at a hospice, she observed that in spite of being surrounded by tragedy, "there were some really beautiful things that the staff did for each other, to support each other."

Later, she worked with a team to develop an outdoor program for handicapped children that she felt was an exemplar of a caring culture. She explains: "We all were definitely lifted up by the experience that we had. . . . And we knew that each one of these kids had had some kind of magical experience, and that something important had been seeded from that experience." The overall culture was characterized by "healthy human exchange." Everyone felt that they were safe and would be taken care of. Thus they were able to settle into their own cycles in a way that worked for everyone. The culture was characterized by humor and play and a tolerance for diversity. As a result, "people were able to reveal their basic kindness."

In the hospital environment, this type of support allows the staff to be relaxed and spontaneous, and it gives the staff members what they need emotionally in order to continue to be involved with patients. An oncology nurse describes her team:

> There is a special group of nurses on the floor . . . yet we're not all . . . great at the same time and we are real lax at charting and lots of other things but we don't bug each other and we really do support each other . . . and love each other. It's funny. There's something about loving the nurses that you are with that makes it easier to love patients.

A team or other supportive context is also necessary in order for caregivers to maintain the broader perspective that sustains them and serves as a resource for clients who cannot see beyond the despair. When a caregiver becomes too focused in or consumed by a patient's inner world, the caring team can offer another perspective, beyond the client's own experience. As the next chapter shows, this team function can prevent destructive kinds of over-involvement.

For example, on a psychiatric unit, some patients with dissociative disorders (MPDs) describe childhood experiences growing up within satanic cults where they experienced and witnessed horrendous abuse and torture. Staff members are at risk for becoming seduced by a fascination with the horror and losing sight of the human element. The nurse manager on the unit uses individual supervision to help staff members:

> When I hear somebody go "wow that's fascinating," I get chills up my spine thinking, oh no, . . . I've got to pull this person in and do some reality checking with them and help them know they can . . . talk about this and that there is an outlet for this.

In other settings, horror may take the form of bodily breakdown or death, situations that most people would rather not know about, never mind be involved in. A larger context that mirrors a life-affirming reality is necessary, then, for a caring spirit to emerge.

Patient-Centered Support

In addition to getting the emotional support necessary to stay involved with clients, being part of a competent team that values caring for patients is also important. An oncology nurse describes how a team is necessary to provide caring because she alone cannot have a special relationship with all patients. She explains that when she is not "in love" with a patient, she is less able to give high-quality input. "I try to find someone who is better able by virtue of that kind of a relationship and I certainly defer. . . . I don't want to love everybody. I don't think you're supposed to or can." So, rather than trying to be perfect and to stretch beyond their human limits, caregivers can relax and know that they are not the only resources for their patients.

Because caring is not seen as an individual achievement, when caregivers have a meaningful experience of caring, they talk about all the resources that made that experience possible. The occupational therapist's metaphor of a band creating improvisational music, which was presented to illustrate the aesthetic nature of caring, bears repeating here as a metaphor for a caring team:

> Each person plays a part in the creation of something beautiful. . . . If the right players are working together and there is the right feeling, it's obvious where you are supposed to go, even though you are creating something that has never been created before, because out of that situation, the forms emerge. . . . It's based on this intuitive sense of proportion, and placement, and timing and texture. . . . It's very relational to what the other people are doing.

A nurse who became deeply involved with the young man dying of AIDS illustrates this shared participation: "We gave him the best that we could give. It was a win for everyone." There was a sense of shared pride. "I felt proud that the institution had supported me, that the means and the resources were available." The team shared her pride as well: "Nurses walked a little bit straighter after that. It added to their sense of worth, even the ones who didn't care for him. They were saying, 'We're proud you are one of us, we're proud of us.'"

Shared participation is also necessary at a very practical level in order for the caregiver to be able to prioritize workloads based on caring rather than on task completion. An emphasis on productivity is critical in health care these days; however, productivity can be rigidly interpreted and can actually be hampered by an overreliance on industrial models of efficiency. To break out of the routine and to spend extra time with a patient can lead to breakthroughs in that person's treatment, ultimately saving resources for both the institution and the client, as was shown with the nurse who rocked the child who had cancer. She was able to rock with that child for an hour and a half, an allotment of time that is highly unusual for one client, particularly because he wasn't even assigned to her. One can only speculate what the outcome might have been had this boy remained withdrawn and unresponsive to treatment. Certainly, in terms of economic and human resources, the cost would have been high, and it would have been invested into a downward spiral, because he just kept getting worse. In fact, unless something else happened to mobilize him, he probably would have died.

What made it possible for this nurse to invest that time and energy in the child was a well-staffed hospital and a team that trusted and supported her intervention. She didn't even have to worry and interrupt this moment with the child to make arrangements for the care of her other patients because the team, as soon as they saw her rocking him, filled in for her without her even having to ask.

Thus a caring team, one that values the human element in health care, is necessary for caring to be carried out. A dilemma frequently mentioned occurs when medical decisions are made, which other team members feel are not in the best interest of the patients, such as the continuation of expensive and painful procedures on a patient who is dying, or the decision to withhold the truth about a patient's condition. In these situations, health-care professionals feel that they are prevented from caring. In other situations, caregivers may not be able to make up for the apathy or incompetence of other team members.

In situations such as these, when support is not present, the results can be very destructive. Two nurses talked about being involved in situations where a patient died needlessly due to the lack of caring by others. In both cases, the doctor and the other nurses did not respond to their concerns about the patient's condition, nor did they follow through by monitoring the patient's condition on other shifts. In both cases, it was impossible to work single-handedly to do what was needed to keep the patient alive. To sustain life required teamwork that did not happen. Chapter 10 shows how this lack of support from a team can be emotionally hazardous to caregivers as well as dangerous to patients.

Patient Participation

The participation of the patient in a caring relationship will help to determine the form of the communication and the possibility of a caring relationship. As has been shown, caring communication does not depend on the interpersonal abilities of patients to engage their caregivers, for real caring goes beyond these superficial manifestations of self to recognize the universality of the person's humanity. Caregivers connect with the person's center or inner spirit. Therefore, the impulse to care does not necessarily depend on the participation of the patient, but the unfolding of the relationship does. The first quality of the patients that seems to affect caring is their ability to respond or reciprocate in some way, and the second is their ability to transcend or to find meaning in their situation.

Ability to Respond

The response of the client, no matter how basic, is a part of the intersubjective nature of caring. This response begins by presenting the caregiver with the opportunity to make a difference. This opportunity may be perceived as the degree of need expressed. As one caregiver says, "You tend to get involved with the ones that . . . need you more."

Once the need is identified, the patient has to respond in some way. A psychiatric nurse recalled working with a mute catatonic woman in the back ward of a state hospital when she was a student, many years ago:

> This woman was curled up, very depressed, very chronic looking, and I would just kneel in front of her . . . and blather on about "I'm a student nurse" or whatever, and the thing that was so wonderful about it was that I did make a difference. . . . She began to nod her head in response to something I would say, and then she began to talk, and refer to me by name, and the last day, she walked me to the bus as I was leaving.

This nurse explains, "The energy has to start somewhere, with one person, but it's the mutuality of it that gives it the power. She responded, that was literally all she had to do."

As Chapter 5 showed, with the woman dying at home of a malignant tumor in her leg, responsiveness is as unique as each person is. As you may recall, she lived an odd "rather nonverbal life" with her brother. Her leg grew to grotesque proportions, with foul-smelling drainage, but she refused to have it amputated. Although she never said thank you for any of the many extra things that her caregivers did for her, her nurse recognized, "that's just the kind of person she was. . . . But it didn't matter with her because she . . . gave us . . . a lot in her nonverbal communication with us. . . . All of us dearly loved her." Her real gift to her caregivers was when she "came alive" and enjoyed herself during a surprise birthday party they gave her weeks before she died.

Ability to Find Meaning

Patients who have the ability to participate in a caring relationship and are able to transcend despair by finding meaning are a source of inspiration to caregivers. These are often the patients whom caregivers remember when asked to talk about their most significant experiences with caring. These patients serve as an important resource for that broader perspective that caregivers have to have in order to sustain themselves and to mobilize hope in other patients who are struggling to find meaning. These patients are seen as special people. "When you see a patient doing

the best with a bad situation, your heart really goes out to them."
A young man who died of AIDS was described as "quite a spirit . . .
he left quite an impact . . . he brought out the best in people."

Patients were often seen as role models for how to handle
suffering. A nurse describes a patient: "He always kept his dignity.
He was always polite, always well mannered and always consid-
erate . . . sort of a role model for me if I'm ever in that situation."
Another says, "This lady had courage. She was grace under pressure." Another was inspired by a patient's "warmth and her
loving . . . when people are still able to emote those kind of feelings in spite of their limitations, . . . she [the nurse] can learn a lot
from that." In fact, as one said, "My patients have taught me my
philosophy of living and dying."

Seven

The Distinct Nature of a Professional Caring Involvement

*C*ommon wisdom and experience have taught us that we should not rush headlong into involvement with clients, blinded by our own emotional reactions. Most caregivers have experienced their share of personal disasters that result from attempts to control or to rescue clients, or from becoming personally entangled with clients in a way that they live to regret. These misguided attempts at helping diminish rather than enhance both the caregiver and the client.

Traditional professional socialization teaches us to avoid these dangers by keeping our feelings out of our work and by maintaining a safe personal distance from clients. This attitude, however, devalues caring (Morse, Solberg, Neander, Botorff, & Johnson, 1990) and removes the caregiver from the emotional satisfaction that is inherent to meaningful involvements (Benner & Wrubel, 1989). Benner and Wrubel (1989) point out, "The remedy for overinvolvement is not lack of involvement but the right kind of involvement" (p. 375). The purpose of this chapter is to make explicit the qualities that distinguish caring as a unique form of communication and distinguish it from destructive forms of overinvolvement.

Throughout, the preceding chapters have made reference to qualities that make caring unique in this way. This chapter reviews these qualities in greater depth as they contribute to our understanding of the distinct nature of a caring-centered involvement.

The qualities reviewed here are (a) self-awareness and purposeful use of self, (b) lack of ego involvement, (c) empowerment through the mobilization of resources, (d) transcendence, (e) aesthetics, and (f) contextual support. Finally, this chapter looks at all of this in relationship to the caregiver's level of skill development.

Self-Awareness and Purposeful Use of Self

The risks of the wrong kind of involvement require a very sophisticated level of self-understanding and a constant awareness of one's own participation in a relationship with a client. As Chapter 5 showed, caregivers must process their own subjective experience of self in the relationship in such a way that they are able to remain focused on the needs of the client. Expert caregivers are aware of their own needs for personal gratification and monitor these needs within the relational context. The counselor who became involved with the young woman with MPD talks about how he needed to be aware of his own vulnerability to becoming involved in the wrong way. As he says, "there were times when I was home and I'd start crying thinking about her torment. I really wanted her to be free of this torment."

Traditional wisdom urges caregivers to avoid becoming emotionally involved when working with people with such a complex disorder, for fear of being seduced or manipulated by the patient. As this counselor explained, "There is a fear that if you get involved with someone you get 'sucked out' or lose it in some way—lose control." These fears could include becoming sexually involved or succumbing to a client's idealized fantasy of the caregiver's attributes or powers. These fears must be taken seriously and explored whenever they come up; however, these fears do not characterize the experiences of caring.

The psychologist who spent the afternoon at the scene of a crime with her client does not hold herself back from caring out of fear of the wrong kind of involvement. Clients may want to invite her to their house or to initiate other contacts that she is not comfortable with; however, she explains:

These can all be handled easily. To me the intimacy stuff that gets you into trouble is in a whole other category. If you were to look at theory being box one, [box] two is . . . where you leap in and maybe use more of yourself, . . . and [box] three is getting into trouble because you've left theory and judgment behind. That [problem of] leaving theory and judgment behind seems real far away from where I'm at. There's a humanity that one has to have in this kind of treatment.

Expert caregivers have an awareness of themselves that allows them to participate fully in the relationship, based on their instinctive sense of what is right for them. The nature of the participation in the relationship will be as unique as the caregivers themselves. Expert caregivers do not have to keep their distance from patients in order to respond in a way that is helpful. They do not have to be objective in the sense that they do not have to separate from their feeling response. Rather than distance from their feelings, they integrate their feelings with their own knowledge and experience.

Expert caregivers can participate fully in the subjective world of a patient without becoming "sucked in" or consumed by it because they have access to a broader perspective. They are able to see a larger picture than the client has access to at that time. Thus they achieve a therapeutic *perspective* rather than therapeutic *objectivity*.

This authentic participation, which is based on self-awareness, is different from the traditional advice that caregivers should maintain so-called appropriate boundaries. This admonishment, which is often given to caregivers in the name of professionalism, is based on the assumption that there is a uniform amount of professional distance between client and caregiver that is considered proper.

Expert caregivers challenge these conventional assumptions of distance by making creative use of boundaries. Rather than setting up boundaries as a defensive wall between themselves and their clients, these caregivers organize and compartmentalize aspects of the experience in a way that allows them to stay involved without becoming overwhelmed.

For example, a nurse who works with patients with horrifying histories of abuse describes how, to protect herself, she distances from the content rather than from her patient:

What I try to do is listen to it and then . . . sometimes I find myself drifting so I don't have to listen to the whole thing . . . , being there with them, but not be there with them during that period of it. Enough so that I can help them at the end.

She creates a boundary to distance from the abuse, rather than from the client. She stays connected with her client at a very human level, what Watson (1988b) would call the human center of the person, as opposed to becoming immersed in every aspect of this person's experience.

Not only does this approach protect the caregiver from experiencing secondary trauma, but it also reinforces the client's humanity as well. As Chapter 4 showed, after her client shared a horrifying memory, this nurse did not dwell on the horror, but instead helped the client to reach out and touch her hand, to leave her with a sense of hope and connection, thus affirming her humanity.

A similar way of relating is described by a physical therapist. Rather than becoming overwhelmed by a feeling of despair when working with a client with a severe disability, she has learned to let go and to distance from that part of it and to focus on the person rather than on the handicap. "I really think there are other parts of the human being that are more important [than] the physical component of it."

Caregivers also work with boundaries in a creative way to limit the extent of their involvement. Again, rather than setting up a defensive external wall to limit what they will and will not do, they are motivated more by an inner sense of integrity about what they have to offer in each situation. If the problem is outside the scope of what they have to offer, they will defer to other resources.

For example, the aforementioned physical therapist was very concerned for a man who had suffered complex problems of living following a shoulder injury. His life problems were so overwhelming that she realized that the strengthening exercises that she had to offer were not going to suffice alone:

> I needed to look at a different picture with this man. I needed to let him talk about some of those other things, and then I also needed, in my maturity . . . realized that I needed to direct this man to other professionals to make a more holistic approach, because me doing some mobilization to the shoulder and giving him some strengthening exercises . . . was not going to work for him.

She realized the limits of what she could offer, but rather than use this as a reason not to care, she continued to be involved by helping him find resources that would be more relevant.

The idea of maintaining the integrity of what one has to offer goes beyond a person's role or job description. It is an intuitive sense of what one has to offer personally, as well as professionally. An occupational therapist often becomes very involved with the parents of the children with whom she works. This works for her as long as she stays focused on why she is there. For her, being too involved means becoming caught up in family problems in which she is unable to make a difference. Allowing herself to become involved in such a diffuse, unfocused way dilutes her energy for the child and causes her to feel overwhelmed and burned out. Thus limiting the involvement in caring is directed by an inner sense of purpose that keeps caregivers focused on how they can express their own unique sense of caring without allowing it to be compromised by going in the wrong direction.

This approach is very different from the conventional idea that one needs to keep a certain distance. In caring, there is no limit to how deeply involved a caregiver can become with a client's inner center, spirit, or humanity. The question to ask when trying to regulate overinvolvement becomes then, "What about this person's condition do I need to distance from so that I can stay connected with him or her in the right way?" The caregiver then learns to distinguish the person from his or her history, disability, or symptoms.

Lack of Ego Involvement

The ability of caregivers to enter a helping relationship without the need for ego gratification is a critical factor in helping them to stay involved in the right way. The counselor who was able to be involved in a caring way with his patient who had MPD knew that he needed to avoid being seduced into the role of a rescuer or a martyr with this woman because he felt her pain so intensely. His religious background helped him maintain humility: "The more I realize I need salvation, the more I don't have this savior complex."

As Chapter 3 showed, caring means being willing to give up the role of hero, to be in the background rather than in the foreground of the experience. While caregivers may have curative skills that can fix or solve problems, the caring skills will empower their clients' own resources for healing or for solving problems. The caring skills require that caregivers be willing to have the spotlight shine not on them or on their skills, but on the patient.

Our culture does not hold out many models for this kind of helping. Usually, the helper is portrayed in myths and stories as the traditional hero, with the focus on individualistic achievement rather than on connection with others. Caregivers who identify with this model may feel the need to take over for patients and may try to do too much in order to feel that they are being effective.

Stepping outside of personal ego involvement also allows caregivers to participate fully in the client's experience without taking the experience on as though it were their own. As you may recall in the discussion of empathy (Chapter 2), our culture supports the tendency for us to want to have experience, rather than to let experience take us up and take us outside of ourselves. This ability to let go of the need to possess experience is evident among expert caregivers.

As one nurse says, "I can put myself in their place, but I have to remember that this is not my loss." The experience belongs to the client, not to the caregiver. As another nurse mentioned earlier, "This is their illness experience." An oncology nurse describes how she got involved with a 21-year-old young man who was dying of AIDS: "I truly loved him as if he were my own. . . . [I] doted over him" in a motherly manner, yet realized: "As close as we were I realized that to maternalize my professional care would be a mistake. He had a mother. I was not his mother."

An occupational therapist sums up the value of not trying to possess or control clients or their experience:

> The real goal is to let the child go and to know that they may not even look back, but the benefit they've gotten from therapy is there. . . . It doesn't matter whether they remember your name. . . . It's not clinging, but letting go. And when you let go you've still got it all anyhow.

Empowerment Through the Mobilization of Resources

Probably the most important behavioral manifestation of caring that distinguishes it as the right kind of involvement is the mobilization of resources, both internal and external, in order to empower a

patient. Acting as the orchestrator of resources instead of being
seen as the most important resource is a behavioral way to avoid
ego involvement and the rescuing that goes with it. The counselor
to whom we have referred several times as he talks about his
efforts to maintain the right kind of involvement with his patient
who has MPD was successful because he focused on empowering
her by "trying to draw out of her the immense amount of resources
she had in her."

Because caregivers do not see themselves as the most important
resource, their involvement is by its very nature transient; however,
this is not always determined by the length of the relationship.
Caregivers stay involved as long as they are needed, to facilitate
healing. What keeps the relationship centered on caring is that the
energy is always directed toward empowering the patient in whatever way is meaningful, whether it is to provide a cure or to promote
a feeling of wholeness during the dying process.

A speech pathologist reflected on the relationships she had
formed over the years with her patients and how she still main-
tains contact with some. What distinguishes these relationships as
caring ones is that the relationships have always been based on
helping her clients to "discover their own power." It is hard to
imagine that a relationship based on that goal would be destructive or diminishing to either participant.

Transcendence

An alternative to ego-involved helping is for the caregiver to
step outside of his or her own experience, to participate in an
experience that is greater than the caregiver. Being involved at this
level allows caregivers to transcend an ego-centered connection
and to become more deeply involved with clients without succumbing to destructive, controlling, and self-centered forms of
helping (Montgomery, 1991a, 1991b, 1992).

As Chapter 5 showed, we lose self-consciousness during this
process, and we experience the joy that goes with feeling how we
fit in as a part of a greater force or larger consciousness. This
greater force or larger consciousness can be understood as the
fundamental sacredness and unity of all life (Quinn, 1989) or the
recognition of a common humanity, shared phenomenological

fields, or universal psychic energy, all described by Watson (1985, 1988a, 1988b). One caregiver expressed this perhaps most eloquently when she commented that she has the opportunity to "experience a thousand different lifetimes through someone else's eyes."

Caregivers describe ministering to the spirit within the person. This deeper connection allows them to transcend judgments and to connect with clients who are unable to respond, whose personality or self is unrecognizable due to physical or mental deterioration, or who may be just difficult to like.

They see themselves as a conduit for some greater energy rather than being the ones who are doing the healing. This allows them access to a source of energy beyond themselves. As mentioned previously, one nurse describes this as "pulling from abundance." Another says, "I don't know how to sustain it [caring] without that connection, without something greater." Another explains: "There is an endless amount of love of God for people, so I don't even worry about that. . . . I really feel like there is a wealth of love that God has given to the whole, to everybody, and it's available to be used. And so I can love these people with my whole heart."

Caring, then, is characterized by a deeper involvement and love that transcends a personalized ego-driven connection. When this transcendent connection exists, caregivers can express their love and their caring freely without having to hold back for fear of becoming too involved (Montgomery, 1991a, 1991b, 1992).

Aesthetics

Certain rhythmic patterns associated with this right kind of involvement are recognizable at an aesthetic level. At these times, caring feels effortless and correct, as though the communication is in keeping with a larger order. When the relationship is right, there is a flow, harmony, and easiness to involvement. The knowledge of what to do seems to flow more easily during these moments, as though it, too, is part of a larger pattern. This aesthetic quality lends an enriching or satisfying feeling to the experience, so that even painful feelings such as grief and trauma are experienced as patterns of tension and of resolution of tension characteristic of many art forms (Gendron, 1988). These rhythmic patterns are then experienced on an emotional level as catharsis and fulfillment rather than as discord or distress (Montgomery, 1992).

These aesthetic patterns are in contrast to the distressful feelings engendered from destructive forms of overinvolvement. Caregivers describe feelings of awkwardness, discord, or disharmony when the relationship is not right.

Contextual Support

Caring occurs from within a contextual web of connection rather than from isolation. This context provides support and allows caregivers to maintain a balanced perspective. Caregivers' personal lives, a part of this contextual support, need to supply sufficient ego gratification and opportunities for joy and pleasure. Otherwise, caregivers are at risk for using their clients to gratify these needs.

A caregiver's personal history is another important resource from which to draw the broader perspective that allows caregivers to create new meanings for clients that lend themselves to hope and healing. While some draw on the resources of a healthy, supportive personal history, others who grew up "on the other side" may feel a special empathy for their clients but somehow have still managed to draw positive meaning from their experience. Without this perspective they are at risk for becoming immersed in a client's experience in a way that is not helpful.

Ideally, a team provides a supportive context for caring, although some highly experienced and successful caregivers are able to create a context for caring even when such support is not available from a team. This is possible for them because their close involvement creates opportunities. For example, some caregivers perceive themselves as a part of the patient's support system. Others rely on a strong personal support system to sustain themselves.

This context of connection and support is another characteristic that distinguishes caring from inappropriate attempts at helping. When a caregiver believes that he or she is the only person who can help, that caregiver has become removed from context. Even when resources look bleak and are hard to find, expert caregivers always perceive themselves in connection with others and manage to create some context to support their caring.

Level of Skill Development

The term *expert caregiver,* used frequently in this text, implies that these caring practices require a certain level of skill and experience. The term *expert* is based on Pat Benner's (1984) theory, in which she has applied the Dreyfus model of skill acquisition to skill development in nursing. According to the Dreyfus model, learners progress through stages of learning that involve changes in three general areas. The first is a movement away from a reliance on abstract principles to the use of past experience to solve problems. The second is a change in perception from seeing bits and pieces of information to seeing a complete whole in which only certain parts are relevant. The final area is a movement from detached observer to involved performer. Benner argues that this involvement or engagement is an expression of caring and that caring, therefore, is necessary for expert practice.

As practitioners progress in these three general areas, they advance through five stages. The first stage is *novice.* Here, the learner is focused on concrete and objective attributes of the patient's condition and relies on concrete rules and procedures. Gradually, the learner appreciates more abstract or global information and begins to think in terms of guidelines rather than rules. The focus in this stage, called *advanced beginner,* is still pretty narrow, however, and the learner does not prioritize well. During the next stage, *competent,* the learner is able to organize and master the many activities of clinical nursing but may still miss some of the more subtle aspects. In the *proficient* stage, the learner is able to see the situation as a whole and can recognize expected patterns based on experience. There is now a response to the more subtle cues about a patient's condition.

Finally, in the last stage, *expert,* there is a transformation beyond the rules to a new way of knowing, which incorporates intuition as well as theory. Clinicians at this level have an intuitive grasp that allows them to zero in on the problems. Clinicians describe being at one with the experience as they are fully engaged and involved. They are attuned to a complexity of subtle information and cues that no theory can capture. Therefore, their practice challenges, refines, and expands existing theory.

All of these stages, however, are contextual, and while care-givers may be experts in certain situations with certain clients,

they may go back to the structure of earlier stages when challenged with novel stimuli and unfamiliar problems. Likewise,
novices may function as experts, given the right set of conditions
that tap into their unique resources and experiences. Therefore, it
is not useful to categorically label clinicians according to these
stages.

The narratives described thus far reflect this level of expert
practice. These narratives have shown how exemplars of caring
communication involve total engagement, intuition, and expand-
ing the boundaries of existing theory. Because many of these skills
rely on past experience and relationships with others, both personally and professionally, caregivers who are new to their particular discipline may have life experience that allows them to know
the experience of caring and to stay centered with patients in this
way.

Some clients will challenge caregivers, especially beginners,
whose good intentions are not supported by skills and experience.
Many of these clients are so removed from their own humanity
that they do not know the experience of an authentic relationship,
and they may try to draw the caregiver into their world in destructive ways. Some caregivers may identify with the patient's symptoms or problems and may connect with these rather than with the
patient's inner person or spirit. It may require a lot of guidance to
sort through all the intricacies of these relationships.

While this book is intended to serve as a guide, it is no substitute
for an individual mentor or a caring team to guide new practitioners through the complexities of each unique situation, or at least
to model this level of skill. Learners need to remember, also, that
they do not need to become involved with every patient. When a
patient challenges us beyond our resources, it is appropriate to
hold back and seek structure and guidance from relevant theories
and protocols until we feel comfortable with a more personal level
of involvement.

Finally, all caregivers, even experts, have needs that are outside
of our awareness, which make us vulnerable to becoming involved in the wrong way with clients. Therefore, all of us need to
realize that our level of skill is contextual, not absolute. All of us
may need the guidance of a mentor, a team, or personal counseling
to help us continue on our own journey of self-development and
self-discovery.

Part III

The Effects of Caring

Eight

The Transformative Effects
of Caring

Effects on the Caregiver

Caring seems to have an alchemical quality, an energizing effect on the caregiver that might be described as a peak experience, one that creates meaning and reinforces commitment. Caring is described as "that spark." Without it, the work would be bleak. A hospice nurse said, "I go on a high when I've gone into a patient's home and done something that's making them comfortable. I come out feeling like I'm drugged because it feels so good and they are grateful." The nurse who shared her own sadness about the suicidal patient in group described feeling "more alive" after the experience. One nurse described her caring for an AIDS patient until his death as "the most powerful, the most uplifting, the most complete experience. . . . I felt exhausted and depleted but with a sense of peace and accomplishment. . . . This to me is the greatest thing in nursing. It's the greatest reward." A psychiatric nurse said,

> You begin to believe that there's some magic to you. I did not believe that, but there has to be some part of me that did believe that. I took risks. I . . . think that if you really believed that there wasn't magic, . . . you wouldn't take risks.

The alchemical effects also enhance self-esteem and feelings of personal empowerment. One nurse said that, as a result of caring, "you enjoy life more." Many of the caregivers reported that caring experiences have improved their confidence and self-esteem; for example, an ICU nurse said, "I think I've learned an awful lot about me . . . where I think I was always shy and quiet and withdrawn. . . . I think I've had to find out who I am and learn to talk to people."

The intense intimacy that occurs in a caring relationship allows the caregiver actually to experience on some level the patient's healing, or the positive effects of his or her own caring. For example, one nurse explains, "A part of them is a part of my heart, and helping to heal them, by bringing them to a peaceful end, or however that healing takes place, heals my heart." Another describes the mutual catharsis that can occur for a patient and her caregivers: An oncology patient who had been depressed finally "lost it" one evening when they were about to do another painful needle stick:

> She screamed and screamed for probably 30 minutes. Screamed and screamed and we just all held her, . . . and after that it was like a catharsis for everyone. She was tired after that and went to sleep. . . . We were all empathetic with her and it was good for everyone as it turned out, because everyone feels those kinds of things [that she was screaming]. We were all outside afterwards putting our arms around each other . . . and we would all giggle, "Haven't you ever loved the wrong man? . . . yea, yea, yea," and started laughing about it . . . and we all sort of had a sense of you know, dear sweet memories of women's lives that we all got to share.

A successful experience of caring is self-reinforcing and energizing. Caring makes caregivers want to care more. These alchemical qualities create an energizing pleasurable feeling that is described as a "high." This surge of energy motivates caregivers to go out of their way to create more opportunities to get involved.

Successful caring experiences do not create the feelings of depletion commonly associated with burnout. Allowing herself to feel deeply for her clients helps one psychologist to cope with her work because she has access to the emotional catharsis that then helps her to let go of the pain. She explains, "If I was clinically detached it would be harder. I can distance from the horror of it by allowing [myself] an emotional response."

Similarly, an oncology nurse says, "I don't think caring causes burnout. I think it prevents it. . . . [Caring is] an unending thing, I never get tired of it." In describing her experiences with patients, another oncology nurse says, "It's a spiral kind of thing and it makes me more open and more open and more open." When asked how she took care of her own well-being when she is loving so many dying patients, she replied, "That is the management of it. . . . I probably would need healing if I weren't open to it." Another, when asked how she coped with her grief after losing a patient, responded that she reinvolves herself with other patients.

The medical-surgical nurse who was deeply moved by her experience in caring for an AIDS patient describes how this experience has motivated her:

> It's compelled me to want to do more. Right now I'm a single parent, I'm in school, but I'm interested in the problem of AIDS in prisons. I'm thinking about graduate school, maybe in public health. I see Rick's face, other faces. They say "speak for us." When I hear a bigoted remark about gays, I respond. . . . I went to an AIDS conference last January where there was a quilt with panels representing each AIDS patient who died. I was touched and more. I would like to make a panel for Rick.

Effects on the Patient

The mutuality, intersubjectivity, and heightened state of connectedness characteristic of caring means that the caregiver and the client will both be affected by the experience; however, the client's heightened vulnerability will intensify the effect on the client. In addition, the patient experiences the benefits of the caregiver's increased motivation and the resultant behaviors associated with caring, such as the caregiver going out of his or her way for the patient. This section looks at some of the ways in which patients seem to experience a transformative effect, based on the stories of caring shared by their caregivers, and it shows how caring inspires self-caring, heals the violence of loss, and promotes self-integrity.

Inspiring Self-Caring

The most striking effect described by caregivers is that when patients experience the caring of the clinician, they are inspired to want to care about themselves. An occupational therapist has learned that if she does not connect with the children that she works with, then the tasks that she does with them will not make a lot of difference. "Caring is what mobilizes the kid. . . . Then you could see them start to get better." As a physical therapist observes, when she gets involved with a client, "It changed their desire." A psychologist observes, "I can get 120% out of treatment with patients when I go that extra mile. . . . When I model that behavior, they can reach down and they can risk being honest."

The extraordinary caring and commitment of the family and caregivers of the young woman who was described as "hopeless" following a brain stem stroke seemed to be a powerful force in mobilizing her miraculous recovery. The nurse who cared for her was convinced that the caring made the difference:

> You could just feel the intensity of everybody caring. . . . It was just something that you get caught up in . . . just so many people pulling for her, I think she understood what was going on even though she couldn't communicate with us.

As you may recall, Bob, the patient who was extremely suicidal, was deeply affected by the nurse's caring response to him. His whole body changed in response to her communication. As mentioned, this patient's psychiatrist later told the nurse that this incident served as a turning point in his treatment. In addition, she heard from the psychiatrist of another patient in the group (the patient who had broken blood vessels in her face as a result of trying to strangle herself with a shoelace). The patient told the psychiatrist, "You know the turning point for me in knowing that you guys cared about me was that one group that Kate reached out to Bob and showed him the way." Kate goes on to say, "And it was so moving that even her psychiatrist started crying in the session, . . . he called me later on."

Healing the Violence of Loss

Another effect that caring seems to have is to heal the pain and emotional violence associated with loss. The loss associated with death or abandonment by others is a violent experience because it involves a severing of connections. Caring reestablishes a deep sense of connectedness, described by one nurse as a "feeling of peace." This type of healing may take many forms, and it often happens when caregivers work with family members to help them grieve the death of a patient. This healing was illustrated in the previous example of the 56 relatives of the dying Hispanic man. She used the heart monitor to show the family how the man was responding physiologically to their prayers. This connection helped them, then, to let go.

The shock and violence associated with loss also can occur in situations other than those involving a death. One woman was hospitalized on a psychiatric unit after her husband suddenly announced that he was divorcing her. While in the hospital she experienced the caring of the staff. A nurse who had been quite close to her when she was on the unit ran into the woman several years later at a social event. This woman reminisced about many of the details of her hospitalization, and "she really believed that if she had not had that experience, . . . she would [have wasted] away. . . . She was in that much of a crisis from grief . . . there is no doubt that she would have died."

One can only wonder about the number of violent disruptions and losses experienced by the 4-year-old boy with cancer while he was hospitalized. We looked at this story earlier as an example of how the power of caring is enhanced by the intense context of health care. The child became withdrawn following his admission, and he would not speak at all to anyone. The pediatric nurse described how she responded to a strong intuitive urge to comfort him, and rocked him for an hour and a half. After that he started talking again and started responding to treatments. At the time of our interview, 7 months after the incident, he was at home still receiving treatments and responding well. The rocking and the comforting he received from his caregiver that evening seemed to allow him to reconnect with his world in a way that was healing.

Promote Self-Integrity

Patients who participate in a significant caring encounter seem to experience a heightened sense of integrity and sense of self that manifests itself in courage, endurance, and a heightened sense of being alive. A previous story illustrates this effect: Recall the story of a nurse who gave a very frightened patient a definition of a hero that seemed to carry him through the experience of open heart surgery. This nurse's response seemed to be a completion of his own idea, a meaning that he needed to create in order to get through the experience. With this meaning in place for him, he went from a state of near panic (and refusal of the surgery) to a position of self-confidence and control that allowed him to experience an unusually rapid recovery.

Another patient, an elderly woman who had been in the hospital for 5 months, "with every complication you could imagine, . . . hit rock bottom." Her nurse tried to preserve as much of her dignity and control as was possible throughout the extended illness. "Any unnecessary disruption of her dignity or independence would have killed her, aside from the medical problems." For example, this patient was an artist, so the nurse arranged to have her paintings displayed in her room, to help her "regain some of her self-esteem and self-respect." As a result, the patient was inspired to endure, recovered from the experience, and has visited several times to express appreciation to her caregivers. This self-integrity also may take the form of becoming more fully alive in some patients, such as the woman with the cancerous tumor in her leg, mentioned in Chapters 5 and 6, who "came alive" in response to the attention of her caregivers.

One caregiver's relationship with a schizophrenic patient illustrates the kind of integration that can occur as a result of a mutually caring relationship. While working as a counselor in a residential boarding facility for chronically mentally ill patients, she was required to stay overnight with the patients. She was initially frightened at the thought of spending the night:

> There was this one black guy that kind of scared me. He was a street fighter, and he had been schizophrenic for a long time [since a child]. He clearly was hallucinating even though he was taking medications because he would stare at me and giggle and laugh and I know [that] he was thinking something sexual, and we had to work through that a little bit, but he was constantly hallucinating.

One day a really hostile aggressive patient showed up and refused to leave:

He knew that I couldn't [physically contain him], and that if he wanted to take over he could have done it because I was the only one there . . . and that night I went to bed and . . . woke up [the next] morning, and there was the black man sitting outside my room, and it scared me to death. . . . I asked him, "Why are you sitting here all night, you must be really tired," and he said, "Because I want to make sure you're okay, and I'm protecting you." And my heart just broke. I mean it just broke, and then from then on I just knew that even somebody who is really . . . schizophrenic, he was still hallucinating, [but] he still had . . . a sense of caring.

Nine

The Emotional Risks of Caring

*H*ealth-care professionals are confronted daily with a side of life that most laypeople may never have to face. Violence, breakdown, death, suffering, and the utter unpredictability and apparent sense-lessness of life-altering events are part of the everyday reality in many treatment settings. As the preceding chapters have shown, those who have the courage to get involved with patients in the midst of such extreme circumstances usually are rewarded with a profound sense of fulfillment; however, getting involved always implies some risk, especially under such intense conditions. Part of this study included interviews with caregivers who had nega-tive experiences associated with caring, or who felt burned out and disillusioned with caring. Their experiences will help to better understand what can go wrong with caring and how to prevent or at least minimize these problems.

These risks are important to address for two reasons. First, these negative experiences may result in serious emotional trauma for the caregiver. Second, the very nature of caring implies that care-givers open themselves up to the experience of vulnerability. Gadow (1985) explains that in order to overcome the objectifica-tion to which patients are often reduced in health care, the care-giver must approach patients not from the patronizing position of one who is whole to one who is not whole, but from the caregiver's awareness of his or her own vulnerability. It is impossible to expect caregivers to be involved with patients in this way when their own dignity and personhood is at risk. Therefore, those who experience emotional distress as a result of their attempts to care may see no choice but to withdraw emotionally from their clients. The emotional risks associated with caring fall within two general areas. The first is the experience of personal loss, and the second is emotional overload.

Experience of Personal Loss

"Every time you get involved with somebody, you risk a lot. You stand to lose something," explains one caregiver. Many of the stories shared by caregivers in this study involve the death of a patient. One caregiver commented, "The things that I remember that are memorable have to do with dying; maybe that's because those things stand out in your mind, life and death."

All of these caregivers felt the personal loss and emotional pain that go with grief; however, in most cases, the grief was also felt as a personally enriching experience. For example, an oncology nurse described how she still thinks about one of her patients who died: "It was really a happy thing for me to have known her, and I'm sorry that she died . . . but it's not an ongoing hurtful thing . . . it is an enriching thing." Recall a similar description by the nurse who became very involved with a young man during the long ordeal of his dying from AIDS: "The most powerful, the most uplifting, the most complete experience. . . . I felt exhausted and depleted, but with a sense of peace and accomplishment." Another began to cry when talking about a patient who had died but explained that she was not crying because she was sad, but "sometimes I think tears are a sign of fullness, and when you overflow, you overflow." So grief did not leave her feeling empty. It left her so full that she literally spilled over with feeling (Montgomery, 1992).

Not all encounters with death are experienced in such a positive way however. One nurse had become very involved with a child who died, and as a result, she was devastated. She now keeps an emotional distance between herself and her patients and tries to avoid getting involved:

Each time I let someone like that come into my heart, when they die, it's just like I close off even more, it's just like, okay, I'm going to do what I have to do. I can feel sorry for you but that's it, you know, when you die you are gone. I won't even remember your name.

Another nurse lost that spark following the death of a patient to whom he had become quite attached. This was the woman who really wanted her hair styled before surgery, so he came in on his day off with curlers and a blow dryer so he could wash and style her hair. He was devastated when he returned to work the next day and learned that she had died in surgery: "Now I come to work and I feel that I'm just here . . . it's just a total opposite feeling. . . . I don't have that little spark any more." Another nurse was diagnosed with posttraumatic stress disorder following a particularly gruesome death, and as a result, this nurse has been declared disabled from being able to perform clinical work.

This emotional risk of losing a patient is increased on units that are set up to save lives. Death on these units is viewed as defeat and failure. The nurse who lost that spark explains:

> You do all this neat work and put all this energy into it and what happens is the patient dies. . . . You know, you do all this wild kick ass pharmacokinetic nursing in here with all these drugs . . . and then they die. It's a big let down. . . . After she died I just, it felt different. You know you just click in with these people. And after that it's just like well, now it's just my job. . . . There is something there that is not there anymore . . . boy you talk about a letdown. . . . Maybe we look at ourselves like uh oh, we failed, we failed them, we failed ourselves. . . . They come in the hospital to beat death.

An unexpected or sudden death in these settings adds to the incongruence of the experience for those caregivers whose job it is to save lives. Another ICU nurse talks about what it was like when a patient he became attached to died suddenly:

> The man just spontaneously arrested and it didn't affect the way I performed, but after the man finally died and I just walked out of the room and I started to cry and I, I worked in the ICU for maybe three years and it's never happened to me. I got involved with him personally, talking to him. I really enjoyed the man and put a lot of time in taking care of him and he just spontaneously arrested without any warning at all and usually, you know, usually in an ICU setting you can follow trends carefully and things like that don't happen.

These contrasting experiences are quite striking. Why do some caregivers thrive under these circumstances while others are devastated? The central theme woven throughout these accounts of deaths is the meaning that is created from the experience. These meanings are derived from both personal and contextual resources and are explored further in the next chapter.

Emotional Overload

Emotional overload can lead to emotional depletion, disillusionment, and what is commonly known as burnout. Emotional overload is created when the caregiver's human sensibilities are overwhelmed with exposure to trauma, loss, and suffering. One nurse commented, "I feel like in 6 years I've probably aged 20 or 30 years, and I probably have seen more in 6 years as far as human nature and the basics of human life, more than most people will ever see in a lifetime." An ICU nurse describes what it was like for her when, following a plane crash disaster, "We had about four or five horrible, I mean horrifying incredible patients at one time and sometimes it's just, you can't get away from these deep sad stories." Another nurse who was involved with those victims describes a similar feeling: "I took care of this one particular patient for about two days and then I backed off and took someone else because I didn't feel emotionally able. I was exhausted at that point and just didn't want to."

The nurse who keeps herself disengaged from patients following a child's death described being just emotionally and physically exhausted:

It's like I can see [the families] wanting to feel like somebody cares but they just don't understand. We see this three or four times a month and when you see something like this three or four times a month for 10 years, you, you don't have it to care. I mean—I don't mean that you don't care, but . . . it's kind of like you close off a certain part of yourself. You have nothing else to give these people other than you try to be nice.

She describes the setting:

It's a very high complexity demanding unit. . . . You could get involved with one and you would have to go right to another one and they are all real complex and demanding. . . . One dies, you clean the bed and have another one that is just as sick and you don't cry over the one that left and you don't cry over the one that came.

Emotional overload occurs when caregivers are stretched beyond their capacities to reconcile these assaults within their human sensibilities. Each one of these situations involves the kind of human breakdown and the violence of loss that only caring can heal, as described in the last chapter. Yet in some settings, the caregivers do not have access to the caring that will assuage these assaults. The nurse who disengaged following the death of a child commented,

It's kind of like, unlike the parents who can continue to mourn over this person that they lost, you have to pick yourself up, go back into that unit, and take care of somebody else's child who wants you to feel pretty much the way you did about that other kid. . . . They want you to be totally emotional. They want you to think they have the most gorgeous baby. . . . It's just like, isn't it enough that you think your baby is gorgeous? Isn't it enough that I am busting my butt for 12 hours without a break to keep your gorgeous child alive? Do you have to have all of me?

Everyone has limits to how much of this stress he or she can absorb. An occupational therapist spent time in Nicaragua but was disappointed in her own reaction to being there:

That experience kind of threw me. . . . I was overwhelmed by the situation, the language barrier, the poverty barrier, . . . kids with lice . . . and with just the enormity of needs that I had never experienced . . . and I got stuck from expressing my caring because I kind of got stuck in my fear of it.

She plans to return to Nicaragua but knows that she needs the time and space to integrate her first experience there before returning.

Again, the meaning that these experiences have for caregivers, how caregivers make sense of these experiences in order to reestablish a feeling of peace within themselves, is integrally related to how they cope with the experiences. However, creating this kind of meaning requires time, space, and caring. In Chapter 3, the nurse who was assaulted by a patient on a psychiatric unit illustrates the healing that can occur when a person is given the time and the support to integrate the experience. In addition to the integrating effect that her concern for her patients had on her healing, an assault support team created especially for this kind of trauma was very helpful to her in her recovery. She now serves on this support team to help other caregivers who are assaulted. She now looks back on the assault as a positive experience that allowed her to grow and actually expanded her sense of caring. On the other hand, when caregivers don't have the opportunity or the resources to create this kind of meaning, they may have little choice but to disengage.

Ten

Coping With the Emotional Demands of Caring

$\mathcal{T}$he preceding chapters have looked at some of the emotional risks of caring, which still leaves the question of how some caregivers have access to such deep satisfaction while others are left feeling drained and disillusioned. As the preceding chapter showed, caregivers' experiences of caring are based on the meanings they create, or how they make sense out of what has happened. These meanings are revealed in the stories or narratives that they share and are derived from resources the caregivers have within themselves, as well as from resources inherent to the situation (see Figure 10.1). (This finding is consistent with Hutchinson's [1986] research, in which she found that the way in which neonatal care nurses combat horror in their work is by creating meaning.)

Personal Resources That Sustain Caring

Spiritual and Philosophical Resources

The most significant individual quality that helps caregivers create positive meaning when dealing with both the stress of personal loss and the stress of overexposure is a philosophical or spiritual understanding that allows them to deal with being

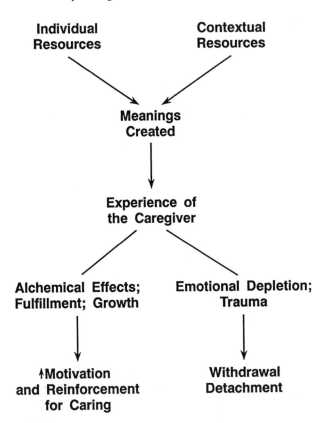

Figure 10.1. Coping With the Emotional Demands of Caring

"repeatedly confronted with one's own mortality, the inhumanity of others in cases of violence, and the threat of pain and disfigurement" (Benner, 1984, p. 377).

One nurse tried to make sense out of why a "very very nice" 32-year-old woman died, when "you see some old codger on 14th and Colfax with his emphysema machine going and smoking away with his oxygen, and you are just like, where are the variables here? It just doesn't make sense." This nurse called this "philosophical doo doo."

Many caregivers, as one noted, "probably have seen more in 6 years as far as human nature and the basics of human life than most

people will ever see in a lifetime." This exposure has the potential
to lead to philosophical and spiritual growth, or it may result in a
gradual wearing down of the spirit. The caregivers who experienced
growth in response to this exposure were able to develop a transcendent view of life that would lend itself to a deeper acceptance
of what may appear to others as senseless, meaningless tragedy. This
is part of the broader perspective to which expert caregivers have
access, which allows them to help their patients create new meanings
that lend themselves to hope and healing, as was shown in Part II.

This philosophical outlook is also related to the transcendence
that is experienced when caregivers step outside of their ego and
allow themselves, through union with another, to become part of
a larger consciousness that lends itself to acceptance and understanding. Very few careers challenge professionals in such a significant way, yet this spiritual and philosophical challenge is
rarely addressed in educational or practice settings.

As the previous chapter showed, caregivers are also challenged
with a significant personal experience of loss every time they get
close to someone who dies. How they cope with this loss is greatly
influenced by their philosophical and spiritual understanding of
death. A spiritual understanding that allows for a sense of connection and continuity within the cycle of life and death helps caregivers to transcend the personal experience of loss. Those who do
not have this spiritual resource may be personally devastated
(Montgomery, 1991a, 1991b, 1992).

The nurse who grieved for the young man who died of AIDS,
yet experienced his death as "the most powerful, the most uplifting, the most complete experience," illustrates how her spiritual
values allowed her to find positive meaning in his death. She grew
up with a deep sense of connection with the holocaust survivors
in the Jewish community and was taught the value of justice and
responsibility to live beyond one's own life. Her spirituality helped
with the loss of her AIDS patient because she had a sense of
connection with the dead:

> I have many images of patients I've lost. They're real for me, they're
> spirits. . . . They pass life on to me. I am instructed to live because
> they are not able to. . . . I have a responsibility to them who died so
> young—to live life [more fully,] to really be aware of what life is. . . .
> We have a responsibility to be all that we can be—to go after injustice.

This ongoing sense of connection is expressed in a different way by a nurse who had changed specialties from obstetrics to oncology: "They feel the same in some ways because I almost cry at a birth the same way I cry at a death. It's so poignant at the beginning and at the end.... It's very alike."

The nurse who described her own tears as a sign of fullness rather than sadness also expresses a sense of connection which helps her to get beyond the pain:

> As long as you remember people, they never die.... We sometimes avoid being attached to people in this business because we are afraid of the pain. But there is a lesson to be learned from that, and it isn't just pain we should be looking at. It's the quality of the relationship ... and sometimes you can't have one without the other. And I'm not tearful because I'm sad, that's not it at all. Sometimes I think tears are a sign of fullness, and when you overflow, you overflow.

She explains the wisdom she has received from attending to people during their dying.

> I got to see this mirror image of myself somehow because I thought, this is what it is like to be dying, to go through all of this review of things, to have the joys and the sorrows capsulized in a form that you can experience in a very short time, but with all of the intensity that you had as you went through your life doing things a bit at a time and never realizing. And I think what I have learned from these people is that there is no right and no wrong way of living.... Everybody does the best they can with what they've got to work with at the time. And mistakes don't matter in the end and really the triumphs don't either. It all melds together into one big experience that has its own worth by virtue of the fact that it has been lived.... I can reflect back on these people and realize that my outcome will be pretty much the same as theirs. All in all, I can't flub it up too badly, and I'm not going to be a saint either.

In contrast, some of the caregivers who had negative death experiences do not express a philosophical or spiritual peace with death. The sense of connection between life and death that characterizes the aforementioned philosophies is absent from the narrative of the nurse who decided to emotionally disengage from her work following the death of a child. She describes how she felt after that death:

> I'm the type of person that if I give you my all, I give you my all. And
> it is just too much, and I don't like hurting like that. I don't like going
> home and not being able to sleep. . . . And I still think so much about
> Judy . . . just little things, you know, teaching her something and my
> heart just wrenches, and . . . each time it does my resolve gets stronger
> and stronger that I not allow myself to go through that again.

She was left only with this anguish. There was no sense of transcendence or positive meaning to help her with this pain. Therefore, she had no choice but to not let it happen again.

The ICU nurse, who lost "that spark" following the death of a
patient could find no meaning in death:

> Well Kubler-Ross's theory is that death is just basically one of the most
> wonderful advancements in life and you go through all these neat
> little channels and changes. How can it possibly be neat? You know.
> It's like, let's get real. You die, you die. . . . How can you possibly be
> at peace with the end of your life?

You can clearly see here the total lack of any meaning that might
allow him to move beyond the feeling of loss and devastation
(Montgomery, 1991b).

Dialectical Flexibility

Caregivers are also challenged to maintain some kind of balance
in their life so that they can continue to feel whole and intact in
the midst of so much human breakdown. One way they do this is
by maintaining a dialectical perspective so that they do not become rigidly fixed in any one position but are comfortable with
contradictions and incongruities.

For example, the sensibilities of caring need to be seen as a
dialectic rather than as a set of fixed personality traits. Every
quality of caring that has been described thus far is defined by its
opposite dimension, and there will be times when the opposite
dimension will need to be called forth. In fact, caring itself requires
the ability to choose not to care, and to have the wisdom to know
what to care about.

Responsiveness is a sensibility of caring that must be seen in a
dialectical relationship with power and assertiveness. Being able

to exercise power on their own behalf as well as for their clients is especially vital for caregivers because the sensibilities of caring leave them vulnerable to exploitation. One nurse found that being responsive and accommodating did not work with one physician who frequently lost his temper, insulted her, and attacked her competence in front of patients and families. Instead, her plan, if he did not respond to the efforts being made by her and the administration to reason with him, was to sue him for slander.

The noncontrolling stance that comes from caregivers not imposing their personal needs or agenda onto patients also needs to be balanced by a feeling of control. This is particularly true in highly technical acute-care environments where a mistake could result in a patient's death. As one nurse said, "As a practitioner in an ICU, you have to feel like you have complete control. If you ever feel like you don't have control, then you don't belong in that type of environment."

The caregivers who are successful with caring are not afraid to take this control, yet at the same time, they know when to let go of control so that they can be responsive to a patient's more subtle and subjective experience. Caregivers who become fixed in a position of control lose access to the human experience and are at risk for becoming dehumanized themselves. Those who are unable to gain access to their own power and control will be unable to fully express their caring because their technical competence will suffer.

A dialectical approach also helps caregivers to seek a balance in their lives that will allow them to feel whole and intact, for breakdown and suffering must be viewed in relation to those aspects of reality that generate life and hope. This perspective requires creating what one nurse calls "alterlife," a personal life that provides opportunities to achieve this balance. For example, a nurse who works with the disfigurement of AIDS found herself seeking beauty on her time off by going to the art museum. The hospice nurse enjoys holding a new baby as a way to balance the deterioration and death she sees daily, and a psychiatric nurse engages in some kind of physical activity to balance the intensity of listening to patients all day.

The enormity of needs that present themselves to caregivers may result in an overexpansive view of their own obligations and abilities to meet all the unmet needs. This idealistic overexpansiveness must be balanced with realism and humility. Educational and practice values tend to emphasize ideal standards of treatment and care that are designed to reach ideal outcomes. The conflict created when caregivers try to reconcile these ideals with the reality of the practice environment has been called "reality shock" (Kramer, 1974). A perfectionistic approach that overemphasizes ideal outcomes and standards does not contribute to the ability to cope with complex patient conditions and circumstances that do not lend themselves to control, resolution, or easy answers. In fact, this perfectionism may lead to anger and victim blaming as caregivers experience disappointment when they are unable to meet these idealistic standards.

Benner and Wrubel (1989) suggest an alternative to this dilemma of trying to reconcile the ideal with the realities of the real world. They describe the ability to "view reality as a source of *possibility* rather than a reflection of *deficits* in relation to prespecified ideals" (p. 395) (emphasis added). The phrase "make a difference," used frequently by successful caregivers, seems to reflect this view. Having an intent to make a difference in a situation rather than to solve all of the problems or meet all of the needs seems to help caregivers focus on discovering possibilities rather than on becoming immobilized by all of the deficits. One nurse says, "I don't think it makes any difference how big the case is or how little the case is because there are always those little pockets of where you can make a difference." A social worker explains, "I have a realistic viewpoint of what I can do—where I can [have] impact and where I can't." Sometimes, making a difference can mean deriving satisfaction from providing comfort or even simply providing a moment of meaningful human interaction, in the face of deterioration.

Those who work in critical-care situations are at greater risk for an overly expansive view of their obligations and abilities because of the life-and-death nature of their work, for the power of saving lives carries with it the danger of thinking that they can control death. A nurse who suffered from posttraumatic stress following a patient's death learned, "You have to sometimes limit the amount of responsibility that you are willing to take on. . . . God didn't save him so why should I think I should have been able to?"

On the other hand, caregivers may need to become more expansive in order to balance the feeling of powerlessness that comes from working with victims. Irving Zola (cited in McKinlay, 1979) once told of a physician who compared his work to the endless task of pulling people out of a river. He finally realized that he needed to look upstream to see who was pushing all of these people in! In keeping with this spirit, a burn nurse became involved in burn care at a larger level, by educating the public about burn prevention and consulting with pharmaceutical companies to improve burn-care products. Other caregivers are motivated to get involved at administrative, community, or legislative levels in order to regain a sense of control by making a difference at a larger level.

Finally, a sense of humor helps caregivers know what to care about (Reeder, 1991). Being able to laugh at themselves helps caregivers to maintain perspective by relieving tension, reinforcing camaraderie with their peers, and balancing the serious nature of the work. In fact "sick" humor may be a sign of emotional overload, as a way to get some distance. For example, on one unit when everyone seemed to be dying, staff made bets when patients would die. One nurse answered the phone on the unit, "Heartbreak Hotel."

Contextual Resources That Sustain Caring

As Chapter 6 showed, caring cannot be separated from its context. A supportive professional environment is especially important, given the lack of support for caring in the larger culture (Bellah, Madsen, Sullivan, Seidler, & Tipton, 1985). Our society's beliefs in self-reliance, separateness, and autonomy make caring a cultural embarrassment because it violates these values (Benner & Wrubel, 1989). As one social worker observes, "A war has been declared on women and children and those who work with them. It's hard to take up a career that's so devalued."

While individual coping skills are important to coping with the emotional demands of caring, to expect caregivers to handle such challenging demands through individual coping skills alone is unrealistic and victimizing (Benner & Wrubel, 1989). Involvement always implies risk, and involvement under such extreme circumstances exacerbates the risk. Anyone, no matter how skillful at coping, has the potential to be psychologically wounded by exposure to trauma. The context must address both patient-centered support and caregiver-centered support, as well as reciprocity.

Patient-Centered Support

Caregivers need the participation of others to carry out the caring. Caring without this support, in the context of a dysfunctional team can be emotionally hazardous to the caregiver. For example, the nurse who became deeply involved with the young man who died of AIDS illustrated for us the personal and spiritual resources that allowed her to grieve for this young man while still experiencing his death as powerful and uplifting. She contrasts this positive experience in caring with another death that was traumatic for her because of the situation. This death could have been prevented. Negligence and racism were involved. "It was a Hispanic clinic patient. . . . The doctor did not want to be called again. . . . I accused him of being a racist. . . . I felt bitter." The team did not support her: "[The doctor] would not listen to my assessment. . . . The night nurses didn't call [the doctor]. When I came on, I started making calls." It was too late, however. All of these failures were compounded by the intensity of being at the bedside with this dying patient. "He looked up at me and said 'I know you're doing all you can, Karen.' I felt rage!" The loss of this man was made more complicated by the loss she felt in relation to her team. "I lost. I lost because my skill, sensitivities, my professionalism were not respected. . . . I was diminished."

In contrast, when her patient with AIDS died, "We lost, but we all won. . . . My commitment to nursing, knowing that I do make a difference. . . . It was a win for everyone. I felt proud that the institution had supported me." She described how the chaplain, the physician, the psychiatric liaison nurse, and others who were involved in his care made such an experience possible.

The nurse who suffered from posttraumatic stress syndrome illustrates another situation in which contextual factors can come together to create a nightmare. Her experience involved another possibly preventable death. The contextual factors were similar to the preceding ones. The physician did not listen to her assessment, co-workers did not follow through with her concerns by calling the doctor and monitoring the condition, and this nurse was subsequently "left holding the bag" when she returned the next day and was with the patient when he died in a violent and gruesome way.

Both of these situations illustrate what can go wrong and what is necessary in the environment in order for caregivers to safely manage the emotional risks of caring, especially in acute-care situations. In both cases, despite their best efforts, a patient died because these caregivers could not single-handedly save a life. The deaths could probably have been prevented, but only if the rest of the team had cared enough to respond. This is compounded by the existential experience of having to be with the patients, look them in the eye, and know that they were dying because the team simply didn't care enough to save them. These situations represent the despair that is left when human tragedy is not assuaged by caring. Participants in these situations are left only with the stark horror. There is no meaning to be found.

Working in environments where technology is not used in the service of caring creates another caring dilemma. Having to tend to a person in a way that is dissonant with the sensibilities of caring creates emotional distress. (This finding is consistent with Cameron's [1986] article, in which she reviewed research correlating moral stress with burnout.) Usually, this conflict involves differences in values between medical decisions to prolong life and caregiver's concerns for the consequences of those decisions, such as the patient's suffering, lack of quality of life, or the financial burden on the family. As one ICU nurse says, "Usually there's just nothing left. They just become horrible, really, misshapen, deformed, there's nothing left, no person, no personality. . . . It's harder when you've gotten to know them."

In these situations, caregivers may feel that they are causing pain, rather than supporting the person during the dying process. This conflict creates serious dissonance with caring. As one nurse says, "I don't like to do things to them that hurt them, and I don't really think they want that." Caregivers may need to detach themselves emotionally in response to this dilemma, and they may be at a greater risk of emotional trauma in these situations. The nurse who suffered posttraumatic stress syndrome was disabled by feelings of guilt because she had performed the procedure that, although medically necessary, had triggered a violent physical reaction that supposedly caused the man's death. No amount of rational understandings or reassurances on the part of those involved was able to assuage her feelings that she had caused harm. As she insists, "Nurses are supposed to help people!"

Caregiver-Centered Support

These two examples of what can go wrong with caring illustrate the devastating impact that isolation and alienation from the team can have on the caregiver. The nurse who experienced posttraumatic stress was a float nurse who therefore did not have a strong connection with the team. "No one would listen to me!" After the death, she experienced a feeling that people were staring at her or avoiding her. No one offered to take over the rest of her assignment for her or suggested that she go home. People did ask her how she was feeling, but she was not able to talk about it because she would start crying so violently that she could not function, and her perception was that she was expected to continue to function.

This is in striking contrast to an exemplar of a team that offered positive support.

> I was there one night when one of our other leukemics . . . got aspergillus in her lungs. It's this really horrible infection that can just eat you out apparently. And she coughed up a big chunk of [lung tissue]. . . . It was amazing and the nurse who was taking care of her was pregnant and we were all feeling protective toward her, . . . and wanted to spare her, so . . . we of course didn't expect her to go into the room afterwards and clean it up. . . . It was just a real upsetting, horrifying thing the whole night and there were people out in the hallway just sliding down the wall sobbing and it was the people who are more on the periphery of being in love with her [that] went in and took care of all those other things and let those people have their crying time and their recovery so, you know, we could all get on.

On this unit, the nurses regularly talked about being "in love" with their patients. This exemplar illustrates the kind of support that is necessary so that the emotional risks of loving patients under these conditions are manageable.

The environment must also address the risk of emotional overload, when caregivers become overwhelmed with the assaults to their sensibilities that were described in Chapter 9. The context must provide opportunities for the caregivers to develop the coping strategy of finding balance to this exposure, so that it is seen as a dialectic in relation to life-affirming events. For example, nurses in an ICU need to be inspired by being able to see the final results of their work—patients who have recovered and are grateful to be alive. Unfortunately, hospitals are organized around a mechanistic industrial model of efficiency where staff may feel that they are in, as one described it, "packaging and processing." While successful caregivers sought out and created opportunities to get involved beyond the confines of their job description, the work environment must encourage and allow for these opportunities.

In addition, the isolation and segregation of the sick and dying in our society isolates those who care for them as well. Staff members who work in oncology need to be given opportunities, if they wish, to care for healthy babies or to provide care during the birthing process. Caregivers also need to be supported in creating the kind of relationships in which they will be able to hear from families who have recovered from their grief or from their illness, or who have made peace with a disability.

Reciprocity

Finally, because caring is an intersubjective experience that is characterized by mutual participation, the patient will not only shape the communication of caring but will also affect the care-giver's experience of caring. Chapter 6 showed how two qualities of the patient's participation—the ability to respond and the ability to find meaning—shape the communication of caring. This section of this chapter shows how these same qualities affect the caregiver.

Ability to Respond

The participation of the patient in the intersubjective experience of caring is not necessary to elicit the impulse to care, but it certainly enhances the experience for both the patient and the caregiver. On the other hand, patients who do not respond, who alienate or exploit their caregivers, make caring difficult. For example, unresponsiveness, as with clients who "shut you out," can be a challenge to caregivers. As one says, "I would take it personally." Another explains, "You feel alienated because you try, you give of yourself, and they don't want it."

On the other hand, some caregivers see this as a challenge. They love working with the difficult patients, the ones labeled as "trou-blemakers," explaining, "There are people who just want you to leave them alone, but 99% of the time you can get around that."

Qualities that are labeled as problematic by the staff are perceived differently by these caregivers. One nurse worked with a "VIP" patient who created quite a stir because she expected special treatment. This nurse's response was, "She was very assertive. I was impressed!"

In any case, the vulnerability in the caring relationship does not rest solely with the patient; instead, it shifts back and forth between the participants. When caregivers are willing to go beyond the professional-role persona and allow themselves to interact at a human level, they risk being hurt. Developing their capacities for self-awareness and authenticity allows caregivers to manage their own vulnerability so that they are not forced to retreat or disengage from involvement.

Ability to Find Meaning

Patients who have the ability to participate in a caring relationship and are able to transcend despair by finding meaning are a source of inspiration to their caregivers. These patients are the special people whom caregivers will always remember, the ones who taught one nurse "[her] philosophy of living and dying." Being involved with these patients is not as much of an emotional risk because they teach caregivers to transcend the pain.

When patients are not able to offer this, sometimes their support system provides the positive meaning that inspires their caregivers to want to become more deeply involved. A nurse who had been treated for cancer herself was willing, in spite of her own fears of her illness, to become very close to a cancer patient who was dying, because: "I kept putting myself in her place, but because she was so loved by everyone, the feeling was a good feeling."

On the other hand, sometimes the family can add to the distress. A hospice nurse described how hard it was to care for a dying woman who had an abusive husband. This woman was miserable and the treatments were making her worse, but he refused to allow them to stop treatment and was undermedicating her pain. "These things are frustrating for us because we can't do anything about it. It's their home."

Another problem arises in caring for patients who are caught in despair, which is very difficult to sustain emotionally. For example, caring about someone who is struggling to live and has not achieved any resolution about dying adds to the emotional vulnerability of the caregiver when that person dies. One nurse who has not had very positive death experiences caring for patients dying of AIDS struggled to find meaning:

> So many of [the AIDS patients] are not ready to die because it's such an unsettled disease. . . . And I think that is why I feel so much more comfortable with the oncology patient if he comes in and says well this will be my last admission . . . and you know you can talk about it. . . . Once you can talk about death and get it out in the open, I think nurses feel a relief and a transcendence, a feeling that I can help you to get through this. . . . [When] my job is to just help with the physical things . . . it's some very gruesome physical things . . . I don't get anything back.

Caregivers who are willing to participate in the client's world will experience, on some level, the same challenges as the patient. It helps if they both bring resources to the experience so that they can learn together.

Even when the situation seems to be without redeeming value, the caring may have an impact that may not be apparent until later. A social worker describes how one apparently hopeless patient now sustains his optimism. Recently, he got a call from an adolescent with whom he had worked 8 years previously in another state. This patient, who was now a young man, managed to find him after all these years and called just to let him know that he was all right.

> This kid came in in shackles and chains, literally. . . . He looked like Charlie Manson. . . . He was very violent. . . . He had demolished half the state . . . nobody wanted him. . . . He [had] pulverized [his] mother, he just beat her up. . . . We had an amazing course of treatment [over] 2½ years, but it was a powerful feeling to hear from this person as an adult, and he called just to say, "I want you to know that I'm doing all right. I'm trying to be responsible, and I'm afloat." It was great cause this kid was going to die, he was just too violent, someone was going to kill him and I realized that if a person like that can change, then the capacity for change is great.

This chapter has looked at the resources that will sustain caregivers as they enter into the world of another during a perilous time. Education, counseling, and mentoring must be available to help caregivers develop the internal resources to meet these incredible personal and emotional challenges of caring. Those who take the risk to get involved have the privilege of bearing witness to some of life's most sacred moments, for there is nothing more significant than the triumph of the human spirit in the face of breakdown and tragedy, or the actual transition of the spirit from life to death. These caregivers are rewarded with continuing transformation and spiritual growth; they are the best guides and teachers to help others make this journey. This text offers some of these stories and insights, and I hope that it encourages others in educational and practice settings to share their stories as well.

Caregivers also need an environment that supports their intense involvement. Institutions must understand that they are centers for healing and caring, as well as for curing. While the curing functions can be regulated, quantified, and controlled, a healing environment must know when to suspend this regulation and control to stand in awe of the mysteries of the human spirit and allow them to emerge. This requires a sense of humility and tremendous respect for those who enter our institutions in need of healing, as well as for those who are willing to enter their world during this perilous but sacred time.

Eleven

Implications for Practice and Education

$\mathcal{A}$t this point, I would like to add some of my own observations and reflections about promoting caring communication in education and practice environments, and about integrating this way of being into professional life.

Reclaiming the Value of Caring

In order to promote caring communication, we have to begin by appreciating its value. Caring has been overshadowed by the technology and science of curing because of technology's ability to create dramatic results and to solve problems; however, caring demands the best that technology can offer and more. As we have seen, not only does caring require the technical abilities and competence of one's chosen field, but it also requires the courage to let one's heart enter into experiences of great emotional risk, the strength to endure the pain, and the wisdom to be able to find meaning in the experience.

Furthermore, as we have seen, caring is an integral part of the process of healing. Alleviation of "dis-ease" involves more than just the mechanical repair of the body. It requires participation of mind and spirit. Janet Quinn (1989) suggests that healing can be understood as the *haelan effect*, meaning to become whole. Healing involves reestablishing the right relationship or connectedness needed to reestablish one's inherent wholeness or mind/body/ spirit harmony. Communication is the most elemental way in which relationship is established, and caring communication, because it establishes relationship at the level of mind, body, and spirit, can become an integral part of the healing process.

Unfortunately, because health-care settings rarely acknowledge or support this level of participation in healing, clinicians who do get involved may have no way to make sense out of their experience. Many clinicians have been carrying their stories around with them for years, never having shared them. Some recall having been scolded for becoming too involved. During the research interviews, some participants hesitated to tell me their most personally profound stories but began by relating a fairly conventional account of something they did for a patient that turned out to be helpful. It was only as the interview progressed that they cautiously began to talk about a situation in which their entire being was engaged and they had acted in a truly authentic manner.

The many talks and workshops that I have conducted on the topic of caring convince me that this way of being is suppressed by professional socialization. Caregivers are oppressed, not only because of low status and pay, but also because their spirit has been oppressed by the scientization and objectification of the human relationship in health care. In this tradition, feelings such as caring are associated with trivial sentimentality or emotionality, which threaten objectivity and control. Caregivers have had to suppress their natural heartfelt responses in order to conform to this detached and lifeless idea of professionalism.

This distrust and devaluation of caring can also be understood as a devaluation of feminine values in both men and women in our culture. However, a recent resurgence among feminist writers such as Carol Gilligan, Nell Noddings, writers at the Stone Center, and many others has done much to reestablish the validity and importance of caring as an important moral value. The stories in this book provide reassurance that these values are alive and well, even though they are overshadowed by the bright lights of technology and are generally taken for granted unless they are absent.

This caring, which is taking place so quietly in the background, challenges the conventional image of caring that is usually sentimentalized and is based on a distorted understanding of the feminine spirit. This sentimentalized image is one of superficial goodness, compliance, and self-sacrifice. These qualities, often associated with traditional views of woman have been devalued, trivialized, and exploited. The stories of caregivers suggest a much different image, involving emotional courage, passion, and highly sophisticated relational and communicative abilities.

Not only does real caring challenge the conventional image, but it also simply cannot occur from a state of compliance or submissiveness, for its authority comes not from any external source, but from each unique context and relationship. The caregiver has to risk the unknown to trust in each new moment and must be willing to act in ways that seem unconventional or may challenge traditional authority.

Because caring is always a conscious *choice*, it is an act of self-actualization rather than of self-sacrifice. The reward, paradoxically, is the release that comes from losing oneself to the power of something beyond the limits of one's own ego consciousness, and the joy of experiencing oneself as a part of this greater force. A further paradox is that, while the tasks of caregiving or caretaking can be regulated and controlled, this intangible surrender of caring is beyond control by any authority and therefore is an ultimate expression of freedom and autonomy.

Promoting Caring Communication in Education and Practice

The vast majority of caregivers do not need moralistic prodding to be more caring. They simply need permission to have these feelings and guidance to utilize these feelings effectively. The message that it is okay to have deep feelings for and even to love clients is met with relief and sometimes tears. For me to work with caregivers in this way has felt like turning on sprinklers and simply letting the natural flow happen. Therefore, the first way to promote the learning of caring is to create the space needed for human feeling to emerge, and to suspend the need to suppress, control, and regulate this process.

Use of Stories

Since conducting this research, I find myself, as an educator, more appreciative of the personal knowing that students, particularly older students, bring to their education. Many bring a great deal of human understanding that has come from rich life experiences, personal challenges, and relationships. Eliciting the students' own stories will reveal the source of their passion for wanting to become a healer. Helping them learn to care means bringing life to their education by integrating the values and science of their new profession with their own unique developing life stories as healers.

To illustrate how students' own stories can be used to teach caring, I share my experience of working with a new group of nursing students who were being oriented to the program and the school's philosophy. After talking about some of the content in this book, I asked them to share their experiences thus far with caring because almost all of them had previous work experience in human service. I was surprised at the depth of their experiences and their willingness to share their stories with such a large group of strangers. Although there were several stories of significance, I use one that is relatively simple to serve as an illustration.

One student described how she would never forget a time when she was involved with a COR (cardiac arrest) in an ICU. In the middle of the resuscitation team's frantic efforts, which were beginning to appear futile, the patient's daughter walked in the room. Ordinarily, the team, for various reasons, would have immediately asked her to leave, but in this case, they responded differently, perhaps because of the apparent futility of their resuscitation efforts, and perhaps because there was something compelling in the way that she asked. After being given the routine advice to wait outside, she said "I need to see my father die." There was a momentary pause, after which the physician told her she could come in. After a few moments, he "called" the COR (declaring him dead). The physician asked the woman if she would like to hold his hand, and when she did, her face just crumbled and everyone just stood, enfolding her in respectful silence. After a few moments, some of the nurses and other team members touched her gently. Gradually, with sensitive timing, they left the room, one by one, finally leaving her alone to say her goodbyes. The student felt that she, along with the rest of the team, was caught up in a different kind of energy, and she described feeling a strong spiritual presence.

This simple but significant story shows that, in some very important ways, this student knows what caring is, and as a result of her sharing her story, her peers now have a new understanding. This story can be used to illustrate many of the qualities of caring that have been described in this book. What stood out for me about this story, and one of the points I discussed with the student group, is the delicate balance of taking control in the service of cure and releasing control in the service of care. The critical element was the team's responsiveness and the physician's willingness to hear the daughter's request with his heart and to be willing to interrupt the usual protocol. However, this is not an issue of protocol or principle (whether families should be allowed into the room during a COR); rather, the issue is the willingness to be open to the possibilities of each new situation.

This story also illustrates the aesthetic nature of caring. We are reminded of the metaphor of the band playing improvisational music. Receptivity and being attuned to the most compelling human aspects of an experience create an aesthetic way of knowing that has its own authority because it is in keeping with this greater order of unity and harmony. No textbook could have told that physician how to respond to the daughter's request or could have informed the nurses and other members of the team of the right way to interact with her.

Through this experience, this student has already witnessed spiritual transcendence. What education can provide her with is a language and a new way of understanding the significance of these moments, as well as other stories to challenge her in new ways.

Use of Language

One of the advantages of working with stories such as this is that they reinforce the passion and vitality of caring. We need to reinforce this vitality because much of it is lost in the language of professional practice, both in education and in clinical settings. Most professional communication uses language that objectifies and distances clinicians from the human aspects of their practice; it does not inspire compassion.

We are all aware of the dehumanizing effect of referring to patients as "the gallbladder in [room] 14," however there are also more subtle ways in which we dehumanize clients and reinforce the mystification and authority of the health-care system. Words such as *manipulative, demanding, noncompliant,* and *resistive,* commonly used to describe patients, reflect our need for control. We have signs that say "Visitors Allowed 6-8 p.m." rather than "Visitors Welcomed 6-8 p.m." Routine charting describes patients as "cooperative" or "uncooperative." When you think about it, the use of these terms suggests an outrageous abuse of power on our part.

Consider the arrogance of putting signs over a patient's bed, such as "NPO" or "Stool Precautions," mystified language that only we caregivers can understand. A friend recently told me that his father thought he was considered a "nut case" because he had interpreted the sign NPO (meaning nothing by mouth) as meaning "neuropsychological observation!" (A study by Cochrane et al. [1992] set out to determine how well patients understood our medical jargon and reports some interesting and alarming misinterpretations.)

I always took for granted the undignified signs that are posted over many elderly persons' beds, such as "Get patient up for meals" until I saw the contrast of a sign a physical therapist had thoughtfully written that said "Mrs. Garcia prefers to sit in a chair for meals." I've also wondered how it might change our sensibilities toward patients if we never used the depersonalized term *patient* in a chart, but always referred to them by name.

Sometimes, even theories that are meant to increase our understanding can very subtly suppress a feeling of compassion. For example *regression* is a psychological construct frequently used to understand "demanding" patients. This construct suggests that the helpless state brought on by illness may cause patients to revert to earlier developmental stages of childhood in an attempt to meet unresolved needs appropriate to that stage of life. The problem with this interpretation is that it essentially pathologizes a very human response to illness by interpreting it as a psychological deficit. As a result, this concept is more likely to engender an objective evaluative response on the part of the caregiver rather than a feeling one.

An alternative term, such as *vulnerability,* can also be used to understand what happens when someone is forced into a situation of helplessness and dependency and reacts by making lots of requests. The word *vulnerability* suggests a universal human condition without judgment or evaluation. It is more likely to inspire compassion, a natural instinct to want to respond in a helpful way, one that will make the person feel less vulnerable. In contrast, the term *regression* seems patronizing. Imagine if you had a stroke and woke up in an ICU, unable to move or talk, and became "difficult." Which way would you prefer to be understood?

As we can see here, words can be a way to revive feeling within the constricting, scientific rationalist tradition of health care. (A hermeneutic [interpretive] analysis of introductory nursing textbooks done by Hiraki [1992] reveals that the language used reinforces decontextualized empirical rational understandings and coercive power relationships.) When we use words that objectify and remove us from human experience, we smother our compassion, and in the process, we suffer a loss of vitality. Therefore, another way to promote caring in education and in practice is to allow for and encourage communication that engages us with, rather than distances us from, the personal experience of the person for whom we are caring.

Supportive Resources

The previous chapter offered a very brief overview of some of the resources that are necessary to sustain caring. More research must be done in this area; however, one of the most obvious needs suggested by this research is for care-delivery systems that allow for consistent personal involvement with clients, and the time and the space to prioritize workloads based on caring rather than on task completion. If this is not done, increasing numbers of health-care professionals will withdraw emotionally or leave the profession altogether because they find it impossible to care in the present system.

The unique existential challenges that caregivers face also must be addressed. Discussion groups and classes, in both education and practice settings, can help caregivers explore the broader meanings of healing and of human suffering, using resources from philosophy, literature, and various spiritual traditions. Healing practices such as therapeutic touch (Krieger, 1979) are helpful, along with spiritual practices such as meditation, contemplation, and other methods that encourage ego transcendence and compassion (Cooper, 1992; Novak, 1990).

In educational settings, teachers can create a climate in which students support each other and are expected to create healthy personal environments for themselves. If students or clinicians seem to be getting involved with clients in unhealthy ways, they can be encouraged to use the list of questions in the appendix as a guide to help sort out the nature of their involvement. Counseling, psychotherapy, and other practices that support personal growth and self-awareness should be encouraged.

Finally, I must add that the process of conducting this research has changed me and left me with a tremendous respect for the quiet wisdom that comes to caregivers who let their heart and soul become engaged in the process of providing care. It is clear to me that the knowledge about caring lies not in theoretical abstractions, but in the concrete reality of these caregivers who are living caring.

The purpose of this book has been to provide a theoretical description of caring communication; however, I am cautious about reducing these experiences to the level of categories and generalizable conclusions, or to prescribe a definitive correct approach. Nevertheless, abstractions and generalizations about caring, as imperfect as they may be, are necessary to give us at least enough of a grasp to get us going in the right direction if, as health professionals, we want to develop ourselves in this way. Therefore, as the interpreter and conceptualizer of this text, I tried to not interfere with, but rather to shed light on the answers that are found in the narratives. The labeling and categorizing of the qualities of caring were done to provide me and the reader with a sense of coherence, but they are not intended to be the focus for the reader. It is hoped that the stories themselves will stimulate the imagination so that readers will be inspired to find new meaning in their work if they are experienced clinicians, and to create possibilities for those clinicians who are just learning about their profession.

Epilogue

$\mathcal{T}$he following story is from "Ode to the Psychiatric Nurse" by Rachel Corday (tape and manuscript available through the Boulder Alliance for the Mentally Ill).

From her room one day, Cooper hears David screaming. David is still a boy and when he screams, it is like a terrified child who cannot be consoled.

"I pulled myself to my feet," Cooper says, "for my voices weighed heavy against my brain like an iron slab. I pushed them away by crawling out from underneath and found my way to David's door. He screamed again in a wail as I got to his room. I saw then something I had never seen on the ward.

"Mrs. Harrington, the nurse, was there and had pried David away from the wall where he had pounded his head over and over, the way he did at these times. Nothing, it seemed, could stop him. And he would keep on until the aides restrained him or until he had knocked himself unconscious. But Mrs. Harrington had stopped him in time, although his blood ran down the wall.

"She held him against her breast and he bled against her uniform. She sunk with him to the floor as she braced him with her body.

"'David, David,' she said, 'no, no, it's alright now.'

"She surrounded him in her arms as if to hold him everywhere.

"'David,' she said, 'no, no.'

135

"Then she came to rest with him against the wall. She rocked him and pressed her cheek against the side of his head. Her face was as if enjoined with him, so intensely was she with him, so perfectly did she care. And David heard her.

"'It's me, David, stop now. You know me. David, David, David.'

"And he became still and his shoulders dropped and his head rested onto her breast as if it had belonged there all along.

"'Yes,' she said. 'It's alright now. No one's going to hurt you. I have you.'

"The aides were there, and someone with a shot. But no one moved in the silence, but stood inside the doorway, their arms fallen to their sides. They gazed across the room at David's stillness, and at Mrs. Harrington as she rocked with him, as if to some ancient rhythm.

"She did no more than gently close her eyes as David's blood upon her cheek mixed with her tears and dropped onto his back and spread into a circle of stain that had in mind some pattern of its own to make. Some memory that, suspended in time, would return and return again."

Guidelines to Prevent Becoming Involved in a Destructive Way

*W*hat is it about this person that I am overinvolved with? For example, am I fascinated with the pathology or the symptoms? Do I identify with the problem?

> (The problem with these questions is that if you answer "yes," it does not necessarily indicate the wrong kind of involvement. For example, identification with a client is not a problem unless it is a destructive identification. Those who are most at risk might answer "no," as they are probably unaware of the needs that are driving the relationship with the client).

Is something about this client's personality or situation getting me "heated up"?

> (This is okay and can provide motivation for advocacy. The danger arises when we get caught up in principle at the expense of the client by making the client a "cause." Another danger is that this may be our battle, although we may not be aware of it and may think that it is the client's need.)

Is my ego getting caught up in this situation? Will this case prove my abilities or worth as a clinician? Have I, as a helper, become the focus of this experience rather than the client? Do I think I'm the only one who can help?

(It's hard to admit when we get our egos caught up in our work. One caregiver explained that she will get a *swelled heart* rather than a *swelled head* when she has a caring experience.)

Can I stand back and look at this situation from a variety of perspectives? Can I hear the team's point of view, the family's?

(If we become too immersed in the client's inner world without an alternative perspective, we will no longer be a resource for that person.)

Might I be unwittingly using this relationship to work out some pain from my own personal history?

(While helping others with similar problems can be a very healing practice, it requires that we have healed ourselves. For this reason, and many others, many people in the human service fields find counseling, psychotherapy, or other healing work helpful.)

Am I acting as "The Lone Ranger," rather than trying to mobilize a team response?

(Successful caregivers will see themselves as part of a team even if they have to create one from community/client resources.)

Am I empowering this person by doing the very least possible for the person so that I don't take away any of the client's potential?

(This may be difficult because it means allowing yourself to watch someone struggle to solve problems instead of just taking over yourself and doing it for the person.)

Do I believe in the inherent competence of this client? Do I feel a sense of hope for the client?

(Every client has strengths and inner resources that have not yet been mobilized. If we become immersed in the client's own sense of despair and helplessness, then we will probably diminish them and create the client's dependency on us and on the system.)

Have I utilized all existing resources on behalf of this client. Have I created some if there aren't any?

(Remember that when caring, you strive to be like a conductor of an orchestra, bringing all the resources to life, rather than being the main resource yourself.)

Do I have a preconceived idea of what I would like the outcome to be for this client?

(While we all have to be professionally accountable for outcomes, to take this on as though we really know what the best outcome for this person should be is arrogant. While we do the best we can, successful caregivers strive just to make a difference for the client, no matter how small it might seem, rather than to try to control the client or what happens to the client.)

Am I avoiding my own life by becoming so caught up with this client or with my work in general?

(Sometimes, when we are in a personal crisis, it can be helpful to temporarily lose ourselves in work, but to allow work to become part of a pattern of avoidance is the antithesis of caring.)

Is there a sense of harmony, or a beautiful feeling, even in the face of tragic circumstances, or do I feel emotionally drained without a sense of meaning?

(This is probably the most challenging question, for which there is no easy answer. You should always strive to make sense out of what you are exposed to and make use of all the spiritual, philosophical, and psychological resources that can help you do this. If it is just too much, then it is okay to back off emotionally and distance yourself in whatever way you can.)

References

Achterberg, J. (1990). *Woman as healer.* Boston: Shambala Press.

Allan, J. D., & Hall, B. A. (1988). Challenging the focus on technology: A critique of the medical model in a changing health care system. *Advances in Nursing Science, 10*(3), 22-34.

Altman, I., Vinsel, A., & Brown, B. (1981). Dialectic conceptions in social psychology. In L. Berkowitz (Ed.), *Advances in experimental social psychology* (pp. 108-161). New York: Academic Press.

Argyle, M. (1979). New developments in the analysis of social skills. In A. Wolfgang (Ed.), *Nonverbal behavior: Applications and cultural implications* (pp. 139-158). New York: Academic Press.

Arnett, R. C., & Nakagawa, G. (1983). The assumptive roots of empathic listening: A critique. *Communication Education, 32,* 368-378.

Bateson, G. (1935). Culture, contact, and schismogenisis. *Man, 35,* 178-183.

Bateson, G. (1958). *Naven.* Stanford, CA: Stanford University Press.

Battista, J. R. (1982). The holographic model, holistic paradigm, information theory and consciousness. In K. Wilber (Ed.), *The holographic paradigm and other paradoxes* (pp. 143-149). Boston: New Science Library.

Baxter, L. A. (1988). A dialectical perspective on communication strategies in relationship development. In S. Duck (Ed.), *Handbook of personal relationships.* New York: Wiley.

Baxter, L. A. (1989). *Dialectical contradictions in relationship development.* Unpublished manuscript, Lewis and Clark College, Portland, Oregon.

Belenky, M. F., Clinchy, B. M., Goldberger, N. R., & Tarule, J. M. (1986). *Women's ways of knowing: The development of self, voice, and mind.* New York: Basic Books.

Bellah, R. N., Madsen, R., Sullivan, W. M., Seidler, A., & Tipton, S. M. (1986). *Habits of the heart.* New York: Harper & Row.

Benner, P. (1984). *From novice to expert: Excellence and power in clinical nursing practice.* Menlo Park, CA: Addison-Wesley.

Benner, P., & Wrubel, J. (1989). *The primacy of caring: Stress and coping in health and illness.* Menlo Park, CA: Addison-Wesley.

Birdwhistell, R. L. (1970). *Kinesics and context.* Philadelphia: University of Pennsylvania Press.

Broome, B. J. (1985). *A reconceptualization of empathy and its role in interpersonal communication (Report No. CS 505 161).* Fairfax, VA: George Mason University. (Eric Document Reproduction Service No. ED 265 584).

Brown, L. (1986). The experience of care: Patient perspectives. *Topics in Clinical Nursing, 8*(2), 56-62.

Buber, M. (1957). Distance and relation. *Psychiatry, 20,* 97-104.

Cameron, M. (1986). The moral and ethical component of nurse-burnout. *Nursing Management (Critical Care Management Edition), 17*(4), 42-44.

Carkhuff, R. R. (1969a). *Helping and human relations. Vol. 1: Selection and training.* New York: Holt Rinehart & Winston.

Carkhuff, R. R. (1969b). *Helping and human relations. Vol. 2: Practice and research.* New York: Holt, Rinehart & Winston.

Chapple, E. D. (1970). *Culture and biological man: Explorations in behavioral anthropology.* Toronto: Holt, Rinehart & Winston.

Chodorow, N. (1978). *The reproduction of mothering.* Berkeley: University of California Press.

Clynes, M. (1979). Semantics: Communication and generation of emotion through dynamic expression. In S. Weitz (Ed.), *Nonverbal communication: Readings with commentary* (pp. 386-397). New York: Oxford University Press.

Cochrane, D., Oberle, K., Nielsen, S., Sloan-Roseneck, J., Anderson, K., & Finlay, C. (1992). Do they really understand us? *American Journal of Nursing, 92*(7), 19-20.

Condon, W. S. (1979). An analysis of behavioral organization. In S. Weitz (Ed.), *Nonverbal communication: Readings with commentary* (pp. 149-167). New York: Oxford University Press.

Cooper, D. A. (1992). *Silence, simplicity and solitude.* New York: Bell Tower.

Cronin, S. N., & Harrison, B. (1988). Importance of nurse caring behaviors as perceived by patient with myocardial infarction. *Heart and Lung, 117,* 374-380.

Curtin, L. H. (1987). A shortage of nurses: Traditional approaches won't work this time. *Nursing Management, 18*(8), 7-9.

de Chardin, J. (1967). *On love.* New York: Harper & Row.

Egan, G. (1982). *The skilled helper.* Monterey, CA: Brooks/Cole.

Egolf, D., & Chester, S. (1976). Speechless messages. *Nursing Digest, 4*(2), 26-29.

Eisenberg, L. (1977). Disease and illness. *Cult Med Psychiatry, 1,* 9-23.

Flaskerud, J. H., Halloran, E. J., Janken, J., Lund, M., & Zetterlund, J. (1979). Avoidance and distancing: A descriptive view of nursing. *Nursing Forum, 18*(2), 158-175.

Freud, S. (1961). *Civilization and its discontents* (J. Strachez, Ed. and Trans.). New York: Norton.

Friedman, M. (1974). *The hidden human image.* New York: Dell Publishing.

Friedman, M. (1983). *The confirmation of otherness.* New York: Pilgrim Press.

Fry, S. (1988). The ethic of caring: Can it survive in nursing? *Nursing Outlook, 36*(1):48.

Fuchs, V. R. (1975). *Who shall live.* New York: Basic Books.

Gadow, S. A. (1985). Nurse and patient: The caring relationship. In A. H. Bishop & J. R. Scudder (Eds.), *Caring, curing, coping: Nurse, physician, patient relationships* (pp. 31-43). Tuscaloosa: University of Alabama Press.

Gadow, S. A. (1988). Covenant without cure: Letting go and holding on in chronic illness. In J. Watson & M. Ray (Eds.), *The ethics of care and the ethics of cure: Synthesis in chronicity.* New York: National League for Nursing.

Gaut, D. (1983). Development of a theoretically adequate description of caring. *Western Journal of Nursing Research, 5*(3), 313-324.

Gendron, D. (1988). *The expressive form of caring: Monograph 2. Perspectives in caring.* Toronto: University of Toronto.

Gilligan, C. (1982). *In a different voice: Psychological theory and women's development.* Cambridge, MA: Harvard University Press.

Glaser, B. G., & Strauss, A. L. (1967). *The discovery of grounded theory: Strategies for qualitative research.* New York: Aldine.

Gordon, R. D. (1985, August). *The search for multi-methodological approaches to empathic communication development* (Report No. CS 505 011). Honolulu: University of Hawaii. (ERIC Document Reproduction Service No. ED 261 419).

Haley, J. (1963). Marriage therapy. *Archives of General Psychiatry, 8,* 213-224.

Harman, W. (1982). The new science and holonomy. In K. Wilber (Ed.), *Holographic paradigm and other paradoxes* (p. 139). Boston: New Science Library.

Harman, W. (1987a). Toward an extended science. *Noetic Science Review, 3,* 9-14.

Harman, W. (1987b). Further comments on an extended science (commentary). *Noetic Science Review, 4,* 22-25.

Hiraki, A. (1992). Tradition, rationality, and power in introductory nursing textbooks: A critical hermeneutics study. *Advances in Nursing Science, 14*(3), 1-12.

Hull, J. B. (1985, March 27). Hospital nightmare: Cuts in staff demoralize nurses as care suffers. *Wall Street Journal.*

Hutchinson, S. A. (1986). Creating meaning: Grounded theory of NICU nurses. In W. C. Chenitz & J. M. Swanson (Eds.), *From practice to grounded theory: Qualitative research in nursing.* Menlo Park, CA: Addison-Wesley.

Jackson, D. (1959). Family interaction, family homeostasis and some implications for conjoint family psychotherapy. In J. H. Masserman (Ed.), *Individual and family dynamics.* New York: Grune & Stratton.

Jones, K. (1988). A message from the ASHHRA president, Kerman Jones. *Human Resources Administrator, 21*(1), 1-3.

Jordan, J. (1989). *Relational development: Therapeutic implications of empathy and shame. Stone Center tapes.* (Available from Stone Center, Wellesley College, Wellesley, MA).

Kendon, A. (1979). Movement coordination in social interaction: Some examples described. In S. Weitz (Ed.), *Nonverbal communication: Readings with commentary* (pp. 119-134). New York: Oxford University Press.

Kramer, M. (1974). *Reality shock: Why nurses leave nursing.* St. Louis: C. V. Mosby.

Krieger, D. (1979). *Therapeutic touch: How to use your hands to heal.* Englewood Cliffs, NJ: Prentice-Hall.

Laing, R. D. (1961). *The self and others.* New York: Pantheon Books.

Langer, S. K. (1967). *Mind: An essay on human feeling* (Vol. 1). Baltimore: Johns Hopkins Press.

Larson, P. (1984). Important nurse caring behaviors perceived by patients with cancer. *Oncology Nursing Forum, 11,* 46-50.

Leininger, M. (1978). The phenomenon of caring. Part V. *Nursing Research Report, 12*(1), 2, 14.

Leininger, M. (1981). *Caring: An essential human need—Proceedings of three national caring conferences.* Thorofare, NJ: Slack.

Leininger, M. (1984). Care: The essence of nursing and health. In M. Leininger (Ed.), *Care: The essence of nursing and health* (pp. 3-15). Thorofare, NJ: Slack.

Leininger, M. (1986). Care facilitation and resistance factors in the culture of nursing. *Topics in Clinical Nursing, 8*(2), 1-12.

Lief, H. I., & Fox, R. C. (1963). Training for "detached concern" in medical students. In H. I. Lief & N. R. Lief (Eds.), *The psychological basis of medical practice*. New York: Harper & Row.

Lincoln, Y. S., & Guba, E. G. (1985). *Naturalistic inquiry*. Newbury Park, CA: Sage.

Locke, S., & Colligan, D. (1986). *The healer within*. New York: E. P. Dutton.

Maslach, C. (1983). *Burnout: The cost of caring*. Englewood Cliffs, NJ: Prentice-Hall.

Mayer, D. (1987). Oncology nurses versus cancer patients: Perceptions of nurse caring behaviors—A replication study. *Oncology Nursing Forum, 14*, 48-52.

Mayeroff, M. (1971). *On caring*. New York: Harper & Row.

McKinlay, J. B. (1979). A case for refocusing upstream: The political economy of illness. In E. G. Jaco (Ed.), *Patients, physicians, and illness* (3rd ed.). New York: Free Press.

Millar, F. E., & Rogers, L. E. (1976). A relational approach to interpersonal communication. In R. R. Millers (Ed.), *Explorations in interpersonal communication* (pp. 87-102). Beverly Hills: Sage.

Miller, J. B. (1976). *Toward a new psychology of women*. Boston: Beacon.

Miller, K. I., Stiff, J. B., & Ellis, B. H. (1988). Communication and empathy as precursors to burnout among human service workers. *Communication Monographs, 55*, 250-265.

Montgomery, C. (1990). Nurses' perceptions of significant caring communication encounters. *Dissertation Abstracts International, 51-07A*, 2198. (University Microfilms No. AAD 90-30091).

Montgomery, C. (1991a). Caring v. curing. *Common Boundary, 9*(6), 37-40.

Montgomery, C. (1991b). The care-giving relationship: Paradoxical and transcendent aspects. *The Journal of Transpersonal Psychology, 23*(2), 91-104.

Montgomery, C. (1992). The spiritual connection: Nurses' perceptions of the experience of caring. In D. Gaut (Ed.), *The presence of caring in nursing* (pp. 39-52). New York: National League for Nursing Press.

Morse, J. M., Solberg, S. M., Neander, W. L., Botorff, J. L., & Johnson, J. L. (1990). Concepts of caring and caring as a concept. *Advances in Nursing Science, 13*(1), 1-14.

Munley, A., Sr. (1985). Sources of hospice staff stress and how to cope with it. *Nursing Clinics of North America, 20*(2), 343-355.

Noddings, N. (1984). *Caring: A feminine approach to ethics and moral development*. Berkeley: University of California Press.

Novak, P. (1990). The practice of attention. *Parabola, 15*(2), 4-13.

Ornstein, R., & Sobel, D. (1987). *The healing brain*. New York: Simon & Schuster.

Pasacreta, J. V., & Jacobsen, P. B. (1989). Addressing the need for staff support among nurses caring for the AIDS population. *Oncology Nursing Forum, 16*(5), 658-662.

Pelletier, K. R., & Herzing, D. L. (1989). Psychoneuroimmunology: Toward a mind-body model. In A. A. Sheikh & K. A Sheikh (Eds.), *Eastern and western approaches to healing* (pp. 344-394). New York: Wiley.

Pettegrew, L. S., & Logan, R. (1987). The health care context. In C. R. Berger & S. H. Chaffee (Eds.), *Handbook of communication science*. Newbury Park, CA: Sage.

Pribram, K. H. (1971). *Languages of the brain: Experimental paradoxes and principles in neuropsychology*. Englewood Cliffs, NJ: Prentice-Hall.

Quinn, J. (1989). On healing, wholeness, and the haelan effect. *Nursing and Health Care, 10*(10), 553-556.

Rawlins, W. K. (1983). Openness as problematic in ongoing friendship: Two conversational dilemmas. *Communication Monographs, 50*, 1-13.

Reeder, F. (1991). The importance of knowing what to care about: A phenomenological inquiry using laughing at oneself as a clue. In P. Chinn (Ed.), *Anthology on caring* (pp. 259-280). New York: National League for Nursing.

Reilly, D. (1978). *Teaching and evaluating the affective domain in nursing programs.* New York: Charles Slack.

Reusch, J., & Bateson, G. (1951). Communication and human relations: An interdisciplinary approach. In J. Reusch & G. Bateson (Eds.), *Communication: The social matrix of psychiatry.* New York: Norton.

Reverby, S. (1987). A caring dilemma: Womanhood and nursing in historical perspective. *Nursing Research, 36*(1), 5-10.

Rogers, C. (1951). *Client-centered therapy.* Boston: Houghton Mifflin.

Rogers, M. (1970). *An introduction to the theoretical basis of nursing.* Philadelphia: Davis.

Rossi, E. (1986). *The psychobiology of mind-body healing.* New York: Norton.

Sieburg, E. (1973, April). *Interpersonal confirmation: A paradigm for conceptualization and measurement* (Report No. cs500881). Paper presented at the annual meeting of the International Communication Association, Montreal Quebec. (ERIC Document Reproduction No. ED 098 634).

Stiver, I. F. (1991). The meaning of care: Reframing treatment models. In J. V. Jordan, A. G. Kaplan, J. B. Miller, I. P. Stiver, & J. L. Surrey (Eds.), *Women's growth in connection.* New York: Guilford.

Taylor, R. L., & Watson, J. (1989). *They shall not hurt: Human suffering and human caring.* Boulder, CO: Associated University Press.

Thompson, T. L. (1986). *Communication for health professionals.* Lanham, MD: Harper & Row.

Villard, K. L., & Whipple, L. J. (1976). *Beginnings in relational communication.* New York: Wiley.

Watson, J. (1985). *Nursing: Human science and human care.* Norwalk, CT: Appleton-Century-Crofts.

Watson, J. (1988a). *Nursing: Human science and human care—A theory of nursing.* New York: National League for Nursing.

Watson, J. (1988b). New dimensions of human caring theory. *Nursing Science Quarterly, 1*(4), 175-181.

Watson, J. (1989, October). *Caring: A core value in health policy—Consequences.* Paper presented at the American Academy for Nursing conference, Denver, CO.

Watzlawick, P., Beavin, J., & Jackson, D. D. (1967). *Pragmatics of human communication.* New York: Norton.

Werner, H., & Kaplan, B. (1963). *Symbol formation: An organismic-developmental approach to language and the expression of thought.* New York: Wiley.

Wheeler, K. (1988). A nursing science approach to understanding empathy. *Archives of Psychiatric Nursing, 2*(2), 95-102.

Whitehead, A. N. (1953). *Science in the modern world.* Cambridge, United Kingdom: Cambridge University Press.

Wilber, K. (1982). *The holographic paradigm and other paradoxes.* Boston: New Science Library.

Wilson, H. S., & Kneisel, C. R. (1988). *Psychiatric nursing* (3rd ed.). Menlo Park, CA: Addison-Wesley.

Index

About the Author

Carol Leppanen Montgomery is Assistant Professor of nursing at the University of Colorado Health Sciences Center and is an associate with the Center for Human Caring. She received her master's degree in psychiatric nursing from the University of Colorado and her doctorate in communication from the University of Denver. As a clinical nurse specialist she provided psychiatric consultation-liaison services to medical hospitals. She currently provides mental health services to the homeless through the Colorado Mental Health Association's pro bono program and conducts educational programs on caring and feminine consciousness. Her research was the recipient of the Common Boundary Thesis/Dissertation Award and the Colorado Nurses Association's Award for Outstanding Achievement.